W9-BHO-492

MERLIN

MERLiN

THE PROPHET
AND HIS HISTORY

GEOFFREY ASHE

SUTTON PUBLISHING

First published in 2006 by
Sutton Publishing Limited · Phoenix Mill
Thrupp · Stroud · Gloucestershire · GL5 2BU

British Library Cataloguing in Publication Data
A catalogue record for this book is available from the British Library.

ISBN 0-7509-4149-9

Typeset in 12.5/14.5pt Garamond.
Typesetting and origination by
Sutton Publishing Limited.
Printed and bound in England by
J.H. Haynes & Co. Ltd, Sparkford.

Has it ever struck you what an odd creation Merlin is?
He's not evil; yet he's a magician.
He is obviously a druid; yet he knows all about the Grail.
He's 'the devil's son'; but then Layamon goes out of his way
to tell you that the kind of being who fathered Merlin
needn't have been bad after all. . . .
  'I often wonder,' said Dr. Dimble,
'whether Merlin doesn't represent the last trace
of something the later tradition has
quite forgotten about.'

C.S. Lewis, *That Hideous Strength*,
in *The Cosmic Trilogy* (London: Macmillan, 1989), p. 375

CONTENTS

Acknowledgements

Merlin reflects many years of reading, travel, and discussion, involving obligations to more people than could ever be recalled individually. A few outstandingly valued contacts are mentioned in the text.

But I am happy to repeat a richly deserved tribute in a previous book. My supreme and special thanks are due to my wife Patricia, who made a truly extraordinary contribution by taking on massive tasks of transcription, revision, inquiry, and compilation. These things were done in an exemplary style and with an outpouring of enthusiasm that cannot be too highly praised.

I must record specific thanks for permission to use copyright material from the works designated:

The History of the Kings of Britain by Geoffrey of Monmouth, translated by Lewis Thorpe. Penguin Classics, 1966. Permission for use of extracts granted by Penguin Books Ltd.

The Once and Future King by T.H. White. Published by HarperCollins; originally, by Collins, 1958. Permission for use of extracts granted by David Higham Associates Limited.

That Hideous Strength by C.S. Lewis, copyright © C.S. Lewis Pte. Ltd. 1945. Extract reprinted by permission.

INTRODUCTION

Merlin is an enigma. He is one of the strangest characters in legend and literature, and all the more enigmatic because there is nobody else like him, no basis for comparison or classification. He changes shape and he darts about. The obvious thing to say, the starting-point for any discussion, is that he is King Arthur's court wizard. But that is no more than the beginning of an account of him, and even the story of his association with Arthur, at least in its most familiar form, is briefer than anyone would suppose without actually looking it up.

Yet for someone so elusive, he has had an extraordinary impact. In the Middle Ages and long afterwards, almost everyone who knew about him at all believed that he was a real person and had lived in the fifth century. That was the case not only in England. His fame was international. Copies of prophecies he was said to have uttered on a hill in Wales were passed around and interpreted. French commentators tried to fit them to facts and show that they had been fulfilled; Italians had the audacity to put him on a level with biblical prophets, such as Isaiah. Actually, no one understood the alleged prophecies, and it is an open question whether there was much to understand. Yet they revolutionised thinking about prophecy in general, giving it a new kind of status, and the revolution continued. Without Merlin's lingering presence in European imagination, there would very likely have been no Nostradamus.

People believed something else about Merlin: he was a magician as well as a prophet. They were less interested in him in that capacity. His most notorious feat of magic, at Tintagel in Cornwall, verged on the ludicrous. Yet by common consent it had laid the foundation of a glorious age in British tradition, the age of King Arthur. It was Merlin who had the Round Table made for him; it was Merlin who obtained the wonderful sword Excalibur. Plantagenet and Tudor sovereigns took this Merlin-sponsored Utopia seriously, and sometimes entertained notions of reviving it. Merlin's presence still lingered in the England of Elizabeth I. It has resurfaced at intervals ever since, with or without literal belief, to inspire poems, novels and films.

Was he real? And why the persistent fascination, even in an age that often reduces him to a semi-comic old gentleman with a long beard and a pointed hat? We can look for him, of course. We can search in a famous book that looks like history . . . but unfortunately it isn't. We can trace him in medieval fantasies of love and adventure . . . but their authors were not much concerned with facts. Different theories have made him a god or a lunatic, or a fabrication of Welsh propaganda.

The Merlin-seeker must face an issue that applies to Arthur himself. It is no use asking the direct question, 'Did King Arthur exist?' There is no way of cutting through the entanglements of legend so as to arrive at a plain yes-or-no answer. We can ask, 'How did the legend originate, and what facts is it rooted in?' That question can be answered, at least to some extent. The investigation may or may not point to a real person behind the legend. The same question can be asked about Merlin. An answer is possible, and that answer can do something to explain his uniqueness, his persistent reputation, and his paradoxical spell – whatever it may say about him as a figure in history. We can go on from there, and follow his multiple manifestations through the centuries. Whether the result counts as biography, or at least has biography in it, I leave to the persevering reader.

I

The Fatherless Boy

Merlin makes his first appearance by name in a work called *The History of the Kings of Britain*. Published in 1138, or thereabouts, this was one of the most influential books of the Middle Ages. It created a framework for a whole body of memorable literature. It established images of the British past throughout western Europe, images that have never quite been eradicated. Yet it was not, as it professed to be, a history of the kings of Britain – not really.

Its author, who introduced Merlin to the public, is known as Geoffrey of Monmouth after a town on the south-east fringe of Wales, perhaps his family home. A genius in his own very peculiar way, Geoffrey is elusive. He was probably Welsh; he was a cleric certainly, a teacher very likely. At Oxford from 1129 to 1151, he was probably attached to a school, though the university did not exist yet. Moving to London, he was made Bishop of St Asaph in Wales. It is not clear whether he ever took up the appointment. He died in or about 1155.

Biographically, hardly anything more is known about him. But his lifelong concern is very well known indeed. The term 'patriotic' might be applied here, though patriotism in the modern sense hardly existed then. Geoffrey never forgot that the harassed Welsh of his day were descendants of the Celtic Britons, who once populated the whole of this island. They had been dispossessed and subordinated by Anglo-Saxons, the ancestors of the English, so that most of the Britons' territory had become 'England', and nothing was left of the rich Celtic inheritance but Wales – geographical Wales. Geoffrey and others believed, nevertheless, that the ancestral Britons had been a great people, with wise and powerful rulers, among whom the renowned King Arthur was supreme.

Geoffrey formed the project of writing the history of these kings, forcing recognition of their importance on a world that seemed ignorant of them. He knew traditions, legends, poems, genealogies. But his researches revealed very little in writing. He studied what was available: a tract by a sixth-century Briton, Gildas, who took up more space with abuse of other Britons than with records of fact; the unrivalled historical work of Bede in the eighth century, although Bede was interested in Anglo-Saxons and hardly at all in British kings; and a chaotic and amateurish 'British history' attributed to the Welsh monk Nennius in the ninth century. But these books did not go far towards supplying what he needed. Then, he tells us, the project was transformed:

At a time when I was giving a good deal of attention to such matters, Walter, Archdeacon of Oxford . . . presented me with a certain very ancient book written in the British language. This book, attractively composed to form a consecutive and orderly narrative, set out all the deeds of these men. . . . At Walter's request I have taken the trouble to translate the book into Latin.

Archdeacon Walter lived in Oxford, and documents signed by both men show that Geoffrey knew him. The book, which might have been in Welsh or the related Breton language, is more of a problem. No one else ever seems to have seen it, and Geoffrey's final production is plainly more than a mere translation. There are clues suggesting that the 'British book' was not a total invention, as has often been claimed. But even if it existed in some form, *The History of the Kings of Britain* is certainly far longer, and covers far more ground, than the 'ancient book' could have done. Essentially it is Geoffrey's work and no one else's, and that includes the account of Merlin embedded in it.

Geoffrey begins by adopting and expanding an old notion about the origin of the Britons. Learned Welshmen knew the Romans' tradition about their ancestry, and tried to carry it further for the greater glory of their own ancestors. When Troy fell, one of its princes, Aeneas, reputedly escaped with a party of fugitives. Divinely guided, these Trojans made their way to Italy and settled there, and the main Roman stock was descended from them. This belief was rendered by Virgil into epic poetry, which put the Romans in historic company.

Welshmen developed a version of their own people's descent that was, in effect, a sequel to Virgil, though without the poetry. Geoffrey embellishes it with family details. Aeneas had a great-grandson, Brutus, who migrated to Greece, liberated some Trojans descended from prisoners-of-war, and led the whole party overseas to the west. After two days' sail they landed on a deserted island and found a temple of Diana. Brutus prayed to her to tell him where the expedition should go. He slept in front of her altar, and she appeared to him, saying (in verse):

Brutus, beyond the setting of the sun, past the realm of Gaul, there lies an island in the sea, once occupied by giants. Now it is empty and ready for your folk. . . . For your descendants it will be a second Troy. A race of kings will be born there from your stock and the round circle of the whole earth will be subject to them.

Geoffrey seems to have pictured Diana in pre-Christian terms, as a real being, a goddess, however Christianity may have demoted her since.

The party sailed on, collecting more of the scattered Trojan remnant, and landed at last at Totnes in Devon. (According to a local legend inspired by Geoffrey but not actually in his book, Brutus stepped ashore on a rock and announced:

> Here I am and here I rest,
> And this town shall be called Totnes.

That, at least, is an English version of what he said. The rock is the Brutus Stone, now near the East Gate. It may really be a medieval boundary marker.) The island where the party had landed was then called Albion. With a slight vowel modification, Brutus renamed it 'Britain' after himself, and called his Trojan companions Britons. Diana had not been quite accurate about the giants. There were still a few, mostly in Cornwall, but after a skirmish the survivors disappeared into the mountains and died out.

Meanwhile the Trojans, or rather Britons, acknowledged Brutus as their first king, divided up the land, and built a capital city beside the Thames, called Troia Nova or New Troy. It was afterwards called London. (Another offshoot: London

Stone in Cannon Street was an altar set up by Brutus in honour of Diana, the goddess who had guided him. So long as the stone of Brutus is safe, so long shall London flourish.)

Geoffrey then proceeds with his line of kings, seventy-five of them. Some are totally fictitious. Some have names borrowed from Welsh genealogies, names of men who lived long afterwards, but applied here to the successors of Brutus. Other kings are taken from myths and folk-tales. But some are interesting and, in their way, worth meeting. The reader learns about Bladud in the ninth century BC, who discovered the hot springs at Bath, experimented with magic, flew over New Troy on home-made wings, and crashed on the temple of Apollo. His son Leir had trouble with his three daughters, and was to be remodelled millennia later as Shakespeare's King Lear. Geoffrey supplies what Shakespeare does not, an approximate date. He also, unintentionally, suggests a riddle: What relation was King Lear to Aeneas? It sounds like a nonsense question, yet an answer can be worked out from the *History*: he was Aeneas's great-great-great-great-great-great-great-great-grandson. Two brothers, Belinus and Brennius, ruled as joint sovereigns, led an expedition to Italy and captured Rome. This exploit sets a precedent to be invoked by King Arthur later in the *History*. A queen, Marcia, promulgated a code of laws which – another surprising piece of information – was eventually adopted by Alfred the Great. King Lud reconstructed New Troy, and it became Lud's City and presently London. His name survived in one of the city's entrances, and still does – Ludgate.

When the *History* reached the point where Britain was drawn into the Roman orbit, Geoffrey had to curb his inventiveness. Caesar's expeditions, Claudius's invasion and all the things that resulted from them were on record and could not be ignored. He managed to cope with them, acknowledging real history, but rewriting it freely. After Caesar he still can never be trusted for facts, but he *uses* facts, or what he would like to think are facts, somewhat more; it can be quite interesting to find where he got them from. He glosses over the conquest; his line of British kings continues; Britain pays tribute to Rome, but as a protectorate rather than a province. Some of its rulers, even emperors, are made out to have been Britons or semi-Britons or Britons-by-marriage. Britons colonise the north-west part of Gaul, Armorica, and turn it into Brittany, a kingdom in its own right.

No one today would defend Geoffrey's account of Britain as more or less autonomous through the Roman period. Yet, by contrast with many accounts, it has a sort of ghostly rightness. During the heyday of the British Empire, imperially conditioned historians treated the Romans in Britain as if they were the only real people there, and dismissed the majority as anonymous 'natives'. There is more willingness now to see the native culture as continuing, and preserving some of its character. The Roman regime had a tremendous impact and Romanised the higher levels of British society, but Britain was not extinguished and native cultural elements resurfaced later in art and literature.

⊶ ⊱◈⊰ ⊷

About the year 410 Britain ceased to be part of the Roman Empire. And here Geoffrey, following the course of events in his own way, moves into the climactic phase of his *History*. He confronts the supreme traumatic disaster of Welsh tradition: the transformation of Celtic Britain, or most of it, into England – Angle-land, the domain of the Anglo-Saxons.

This began to happen in the fifth century, but the actual process is still a matter of dispute. Historians – including, unfortunately, authors of schoolbooks – used to picture an invincible Germanic horde pouring in across the North Sea, slaughtering the effete British natives, and driving the panic-stricken remnant into Wales and Cornwall, all within a generation or so. The extraordinary thing about this nonsense is its persistence, even though the Anglo-Saxons' own Chronicle disproves it.

In the early aftermath of the break with Rome, the Britons seem to have maintained something like the Roman system, though regional 'strong men' were soon making themselves felt. However, the island was beset by raiding barbarians – the Irish in the west, Picts in the north, Angles and Saxons in the east – and, after many years of being weaponless by Roman decree, it lacked the military resources to fight them all. A governing council, presided over by a sort of high king called Vortigern (this means 'over-chief' and may be a title rather than a name), allowed Angles, Saxons, Jutes and associated tribes to settle in the country as auxiliaries or 'federates', who were allotted land and supplies in return for keeping order and repelling other barbarians.

Many more followed the first groups. The Britons could not keep all of them supplied, and a revolt followed, with widespread raiding and possibly unauthorised land-taking. Under new leadership the Britons at last recovered, and partially stabilised the situation. They still vastly outnumbered their tormentors. (Since the question is inevitable, it may be said here that the legend of Arthur is rooted in this period of revival.) During the sixth century the balance of population shifted in favour of the new people. They multiplied; they encroached further. The formation of regional Anglo-Saxon kingdoms and their eventual coalescence into 'England' proceeded, but it took centuries.

The Welsh, though they too split into small kingdoms, retained their independence. They cherished traditions of the catastrophe and the brief heroic age that supposedly followed. Vortigern became an arch-villain, and the people whom he iniquitously welcomed became, simply, Saxons. Whether or not Geoffrey had an 'ancient book', he certainly read authors who gave him information about the disaster – the aforesaid Gildas, Bede and Nennius – and his dramatic fictionalisation was accepted as history through most of the Middle Ages. There was nothing to refute it.

His version begins in the chaos of the early fifth century. He tells his readers that the Archbishop of London, aware that the Little Britain in Armorica was in a sounder condition than the island, crossed the Channel and urged the Breton king, Aldroenus, to take charge of the parent country. The king's brother Constantine sailed over with two thousand soldiers and landed at Totnes, like Brutus and other characters in the *History*. He enlarged his force by enrolling Britons on the spot, and dispersed the barbarian marauders. An assembly at Silchester, a Roman town, made Constantine king. He had three sons: Constans, who entered a monastery; Aurelius Ambrosius; and Uther. Constantine and his elder sons are historical figures, reshaped by Geoffrey in his own style. He plants Uther to be the father of Arthur.

Constantine reigned in peace for ten years. But the defeated Picts became dangerous again because they had a secret ally at the British court, Vortigern the Thin (here he is), the unscrupulous overlord of the Gewissei in south-east Wales.

Perhaps with his connivance, a Pict assassinated Constantine. Vortigern exploited the murder. He persuaded Constantine's eldest son, the monk Constans, to leave his monastery and assume the kingship as the legitimate heir. Constans was entirely unfitted to the role, and became a puppet in Vortigern's hands. The plotter then installed friends of his own in key positions. He recruited a hundred Picts as his bodyguard and bribed them to clamour for his own coronation. They killed Constans, and Vortigern took the crown. Constans's brother Aurelius should have reigned, with Uther next in line, but both the princes were young and in the care of a guardian, who hurried them off to Brittany out of Vortigern's reach. The usurper knew that they would soon be old enough to return to Britain. Like Macbeth, he could never feel secure while a potential challenger lived, let alone two of them. His scheming had made enemies, and the princes would certainly find support.

In the fourth year of Vortigern's reign, while he was visiting Canterbury, three foreign longships landed on the Kentish coast. The newcomers were Saxon exiles, led by two brothers, Hengist and Horsa. They asked to be taken to the king, and offered him their services. He was impressed by their stature and martial bearing. Although he regretted their paganism (they explained that they worshipped Woden and Freia), he accepted them as auxiliaries and allotted lands in Thanet and Lincolnshire for them and their followers.

Hengist, at first, kept his side of the bargain and fought the barbarians who were harassing Britain again. But he was more astute than Vortigern, and realised that the king's weaknesses and apprehensions could be manipulated. With Vortigern's approval, he imported more Saxons from the continent. As soon as they were safely in Britain, he held a banquet at which his beautiful daughter Renwein was present. She handed Vortigern a goblet of wine, saying 'Was hail!' Prompted by his interpreter, he gave the correct response, 'Drinc hail!' His first wife, by whom he had adult sons, was dead, and Renwein's father perceived that he was ripe for an elderly infatuation. Hengist offered him her hand in marriage in return for more territory. Vortigern duly handed over the whole of Kent, without even informing its regional ruler. Saxons were now flooding into the country, not simply as auxiliaries but as settlers, bringing wives and families. Vortigern fell more and more under Hengist's control. Many of his subjects were turning against him, as a friend of the heathen foreigners, who were already having sexual relations with British women.

The king's eldest son, Vortimer, was horrified by all these developments, not least by his father's Saxon marriage. He rebelled, and allowed fellow-rebels to make him a rival sovereign. At the head of his supporters he won four battles. The Saxon warriors fled to their ships and put to sea, though they left their families behind, indicating that they had no serious intention of going for good. Vortimer's stepmother Renwein poisoned him (a Saxon atrocity which Geoffrey introduces too often, in order to get a character off the stage). As he lay dying, Vortimer asked his followers to build a pyramid at the place where the Saxons usually landed, and place his body on top. Superstitious dread of the man who had beaten them might cause them to hesitate. However, his wish was not carried out and he was buried in London.

Hengist's horde reassembled, stronger than ever. Talking of a new treaty, he invited Vortigern and his nobles to a peace conference near Amesbury. The Britons, somewhat naively, trusted him and arrived unarmed. The Saxons hid daggers in their boots and, at a signal from Hengist, killed more than three hundred of the nobles, whose bodies were dumped in a mass grave on Salisbury Plain. Hengist threatened the king himself and extorted more territory. The Saxons seized London, York, Lincoln and Winchester, and roamed about the country at will, wrecking and pillaging.

Vortigern, driven to desperation, consulted soothsayers – by courtesy, magicians. They advised him to give up the attempt to control his kingdom, and instead to build himself an impregnable stronghold in some remote place, where he could at least survive. After considering several possible sites, he tried Snowdonia and picked out the hill-fort now known as Dinas Emrys.

Dinas Emrys is in the valley of Nant Gwynant near Beddgelert, and 3 miles south of Snowdon. The fort is on a rocky height, a little apart from neighbouring hills. Its ramparts defend a fairly level summit enclosure, about 800 by 500 feet. The original entrance is on the west, where it is possible to climb to the plateau through three lines of earthworks, but access is easier – though not much – on the east; here, a footpath of sorts runs along a ridge.

Vortigern brought his counsellors and magicians to the chosen site, and gathered masons and other skilled workers from different parts of the country, together with stones and timber as building materials. It must be supposed that in those days there was some way of getting such materials up the hill. The logistic problem was solved, the problem of construction was not. Vortigern ordered his team to build a tower for him. They laid the foundations, and then laid them again, but after several days they had achieved nothing. Every time the base of the tower began to take shape, it fell to pieces, and all the materials vanished into the earth. Since the professionals could offer no explanation, Vortigern consulted his magicians again.

But then something totally unexpected happened. . . .

━━━ ⋈ ❖ ⋈ ━━━

While Geoffrey was spinning pseudo-history out of unpromising matter, he was also taking an interest in prophecy – specifically, Welsh prophecy. In his time the Welsh were unique among western nations in having a lively prophetic tradition, not necessarily of prophecy as prediction, but of prophecy as inspired utterance, which might or might not be predictive. It had a recognised kinship with the poetic inspiration of bards, called *awen*. Men and women who had the gift went into trances and poured out oracular sayings. These might be simply responses to inquirers, making the activity a kind of fortune-telling, but sometimes they did foreshadow the future, even the political future. Occasionally such prophecies, however cryptic, were remembered and recorded.

A famous poem composed about 930, and preserved in writing, treated this public prophecy with special respect. Called *Armes Prydein*, 'The Omen of Britain', it put together various hopeful forecasts of English decline and British recovery. In the upshot it turned out to be too optimistic. When it came to an actual battle, the English king Athelstan routed the Welsh and their allies. But it could always be taken up again, and reinterpreted.

Geoffrey read 'The Omen of Britain' and noted that one of its prophecies was attributed to someone called Myrddin, who plainly had a long-standing reputation. There was nothing in the poem to show who Myrddin was, but he was understood to have lived several centuries before. Other prophecies, mostly obscure or fragmentary, also had his name attached to them. Geoffrey made a collection of Myrddin material, with prophetic items from other sources. Setting the *History* aside for a while, he combined his collection with a large body of 'prophecy' that he made up himself, and gave the result to the public in 1135.

In the course of doing so, he took a momentous step. He realised that 'Myrddin' would be rendered 'Merdinus' in Latin, which for many prospective Norman-French readers would suggest *merde*, a dirty word. So he changed 'Myrddin' to 'Merlin'. In this almost accidental way, a new name entered literature, one that was destined to have an impact that neither Geoffrey nor anybody else could have anticipated.

Geoffrey had no intention of leaving his 'Prophecies of Merlin' as an isolated pamphlet. That would have spelt oblivion. They should go bodily into the *History* itself, and Merlin should be brought into it to speak them. He took up the *History* again and carried it further, to a place where he could introduce the prophet in person.

He reached that place when he told how Vortigern's tower collapsed, and the usurper consulted his magicians. Alarmingly, Geoffrey says, they told him that he must kill a boy and sprinkle his blood on the stones and mortar. Then the foundation would hold firm. This advice is not simply a macabre fiction out of Geoffrey's imagination. It reflects a tradition of ancient druidic practice. Archaeologists at Cadbury Castle in Somerset unearthed the skeleton of a young man, folded up and crammed into a hole under the rampart, apparently to give it magical support. However, Vortigern's magicians added a stipulation that seemed to nullify the whole idea, perhaps so that they would not be discredited by another collapse. The victim must be a boy who had no father.

Vortigern sent out messengers in all directions to look for a boy with this bizarre qualification. One party arrived in Carmarthen – or, to be precise, the town later given that name – and saw two lads quarrelling. One of them was shouting abuse and boasting of having royal blood; as for the other, no one knew who he was, for he never had a father. The name of the fatherless one was Merlin. The messengers spoke to him and made inquiries. It was true that nobody knew of any father. Merlin's mother was a daughter of a king of Demetia (otherwise Dyfed) and lived with a community of nuns in St Peter's church, where an illicit intrigue would have been difficult.

The governor of the town agreed to send Merlin and his mother to Vortigern. When they arrived at Dinas Emrys, Vortigern treated the mother with the courtesy due to a princess, and asked how she had come to conceive her son. She swore that she had had no sexual relations in the ordinary sense. But when she was in her room at the convent, a being used to come to her in the form of a handsome young man, stay for a while and then vanish. This happened repeatedly. Sometimes he talked with her while he was invisible, and when that happened, he had intercourse with her. After several such occurrences she became pregnant.

Vortigern was impressed by her manifest honesty. He had with him a scholar named Maugantius, who was an expert in mysteries of this type. Vortigern questioned Maugantius, who replied that the case was not unprecedented:

> Between the moon and the earth live spirits whom we call incubus demons. They have partly the nature of men and partly that of angels, and when they wish they assume mortal shapes and have intercourse with women. It is

possible that one of them appeared to this woman and begot the lad in her.

Merlin, who was listening, asked the king why he and his mother had been brought there. Vortigern explained about the proposal to sacrifice him, not even as a religious act, but for purely structural reasons. The boy was unperturbed. He asked to see the royal magicians, saying he would show that they did not know what they were talking about. Vortigern summoned them and ordered them to sit at Merlin's feet. He already suspected that strange things were liable to happen when the boy was present.

Merlin asked the magicians what lay beneath the foundation, since obviously something had been unsettling it. They were terrified and said nothing. He turned to Vortigern, and told him to send for his workmen and have them dig. Under the foundations they would find a subterranean pool, and that was what made the ground unsteady. The workmen dug and found the pool. That, however, was only the beginning. What followed would be far more surprising. Merlin asked the magicians what was under the water. Again they had nothing to say. He told Vortigern to have the pool drained, and its secret would come to light. At the bottom they would find two hollow stones forming a kind of container, and inside would be two sleeping dragons.

So it turned out. The king and the onlookers were amazed, and realised that the boy had something more than mortal about him. Moreover, the dragons were alive and did not keep still; the draining operation had roused them. One was white, the other was red. They fought, breathing out fire. The white dragon drove the red one to the edge of the pool, but the red dragon recovered and thrust the white one back.

2

prophecy transformed

Such is Merlin's debut in *The History of the Kings of Britain*. It leads into the outpouring of prophecy which Geoffrey attributes to him and incorporates at this point. Merlin is definitely a teenager, not a bearded ancient. However, this episode is not a mere fantasy concocted by Geoffrey. In keeping with his habitual practice, he is making use of older material, improving it and adapting it to suit his intentions. Here, the older material is in the aforementioned book ascribed to the ninth-century monk Nennius. His early version supplies a bald account of Vortigern's problem with the tower, the intended sacrifice and the discovery of the fatherless boy, though his origin is left obscure. The vessels are found in the pool and the two creatures emerge. They are called 'worms', but folklore dragons are sometimes called so, and in their confinement they must have been quite small. The red one drives away the white. This is the tale which Geoffrey's introduction of Merlin as the young prophet has elaborated.

Nennius does not give the boy that name. Through most of the passage he is anonymous, but near the end he tells Vortigern that he is called Ambrosius – in Welsh, Emrys. Nennius may only be guessing at an etymology for the hill's name. To give his derivation a little substance, he has Vortigern depart and leave Ambrosius in possession. He implies that in later life the boy became Ambrosius Aurelianus (Emrys Gwledig, Emrys the Overlord), a fifth-century British leader whom he mentions elsewhere. However, he may be bringing this leader in simply because this is the only Ambrosius he can think of.

Certainly the identification will not stand up. Elsewhere, Nennius himself gives the real Ambrosius a totally incompatible dating. Nothing connects him with North Wales; he does not figure anywhere in local legends or place-name lore; and the suggestion that the British commander-in-chief had prophetic powers is grotesque. While Geoffrey follows Nennius quite closely through the main story, he knows the equation does not work, and he brings Ambrosius Aurelianus into the *History* somewhere else in an entirely different role. He does try to account for the place-name – so far as he cares to try – by explaining that 'Ambrosius' was another name for Merlin; and, rightly or wrongly, subsequent Welsh bards accepted that 'Merlinus Ambrosius' was the full name of the seer who confronted Vortigern and spoke the prophecies.

The oddest thing in all this is the disclosure that establishes his credentials. It might not have been difficult to guess the reason for the foundation's subsidence – that is, the subterranean pool. But the motif of dormant dragons in a submerged stone casing on top of a hill is bizarre. Small when lying asleep, they expand and fight when released. The whole picture seems alien to mantic convention and even fairy-tale logic. Somehow Merlin knows that the dragons are there, and overawes the king and his entourage by proving it. But how are they supposed to have got there? The question might be dismissed as unanswerable, yet – strangest of all – the answer exists. It takes us into a realm of mythology, pointing to mysteries behind Geoffrey's feats of imagination, even when he makes them quasi-historical.

The secret of the dragons is in the medieval collection of Welsh stories called the *Mabinogion*. The two creatures were incarcerated by Lludd, the ruler of Britain a very long time ago. Geoffrey knows about him, and puts him in his own book quasi-historically as King Lud, the last undisputed British sovereign before the Roman invasion. This king, he says, had a special fondness for London, and remodelled it with a new majesty. Lud survives in urban mythology as one of Geoffrey's creative successes: Ludgate Hill, the approach to St Paul's Cathedral, is named after him.

But Geoffrey sheds no light on the origin of the dragons. The author of the *Mabinogion* version of this reign has read the *History*, and summarises the London paragraph. Then, however, he goes on to mythical themes of immemorial age which Geoffrey has made no attempt to handle; even he would have found it difficult to transmute them into his own kind of narrative. And it is just there that the dragons first show themselves.

According to the *Mabinogion*, Lludd had a wise brother named Llevelys, who became king of what is now France. Lludd's reign in Britain was troubled by several 'plagues' or afflictions. One was an invasion by alien beings, a kind of malignant fairy-folk called the Coranieid. They could hear any speech that was carried on the wind, however faintly, and could thus eavesdrop at a distance and learn an opponent's plans, so Lludd could see no way of defeating them. Another 'plague' was a horrible shriek that rang across the country each May-eve and drove people out of their minds; no one could find what it was that shrieked.

Lludd decided to ask his brother's advice, and they conferred aboard a ship in the Channel. Llevelys had a bronze speaking-tube made, so that they could talk through it without alerting the Coranieid. When they tested it, a small demon got inside and scrambled the words, but Llevelys washed him out with wine, so that the tube functioned properly.

Then he told Lludd how to thwart the aliens. Insects of a certain species were poisonous to them, but harmless to Britons, so he should mash some of those insects in water to make a lethal spray. As for the annual shriek, it was emitted by a British dragon under attack from a foreign one. Lludd should find the exact centre of Britain and have a pit dug at that spot. Into this he should lower a tub full of highest-quality mead with a silk cover over it. When the dragons next grew tired of fighting, they would turn into piglets, fall on the cover, and drag it down into the mead. They would drink themselves into a stupor. Lludd should then wrap them up, lock them in a stone container, and bury it in the strongest place in Britain.

Lludd went home and prepared the infusion of insects, which, as his brother had promised, destroyed the Coranieid. Then he had his kingdom measured, and came to the rather odd conclusion that its centre was at the future site of Oxford. He put the intoxicant tub in place. At a moment of relaxation the dragons changed and fell into it as predicted. He took them to the Snowdonian hill-fort afterwards named Dinas Emrys, and buried them there in their stone container. There they remained in suspended animation. Having disposed of Britain's plagues, Lludd reigned peacefully and prosperously.

That was how the dragons got there. The story still fails to show how Merlin could have known all this centuries later. Some local tradition of Lludd's activities could presumably have been handed down. Turning, however, from fiction to reality, we can note a few facts about the hill.

Archaeologically, Dinas Emrys is unusual and interesting. Though pre-Roman, it was inhabited in the Roman period. There is evidence of iron-working, and there is even a pool, though with no reptilian traces in it. The pool is close to the stone foundation of a Roman building, and seems to have been artificial, intended, perhaps, as a cistern. In a swampy hollow is a sort of platform of level ground, where someone lived in the fifth century, as shown by fragments of imported pottery, of the types first identified at Tintagel which began to open up the 'Arthurian' period. The fifth-century resident enjoyed a certain degree of wealth and comfort. Amulets with 'alpha-omega' and 'chi-rho' monograms attest a Christian presence, though the Christian was not necessarily the chief householder. The remains of a tower are, regrettably, unrelated; they belong to the twelfth century.

Nevertheless, a person of some importance was at Dinas Emrys at approximately the right time to fit the story. The visible signs do not take us further, or shed any light on the hill-fort's name. However, they reveal someone around whom traditions could have gathered. In later legend the belief that Merlin stayed at Dinas Emrys persists, though he is never said to have made it a permanent home. He left behind a golden cauldron containing treasure, hiding it in a cave and blocking the entrance with a large rock and a mound of earth. The treasure is meant for a particular person, who is identified only as a youth with yellow hair and blue eyes. When he is near the spot, a bell will ring and the barrier will crumble as he sets foot on it. The bell has not rung yet. Treasure-seekers who have looked for the cave have been frightened off, it is said, by thunderstorms and other portents.

When Merlin was beside the drained pool, saved from death by his revelation of the dragons, Vortigern watched the creatures fight and asked what it meant. Describing Merlin's response, Geoffrey at once distinguishes him from all mere soothsayers and crystal-gazers, and transforms what he takes from Nennius. He has already dropped a hint by saying that the bystanders, amazed at the lad's knowledge, sensed a *numen* in him. *Numen* carries a suggestion of indwelling divinity, or, at any rate, superhumanity. The *numen* of Merlin does not belong to him as a person. When the king questions him about the dragons, he bursts into tears and . . . *spiritum hausit prophetie*. The curious and significant verb here is *hausit*. A fair translation would be 'imbibed', if it could be taken seriously enough. The best rendering of the sentence is a paraphrase: 'he drew the spirit of prophecy into him'. The *numen* or *spiritus* is distinct from the human individual through whom it speaks, as will appear more fully further on; it can be invited, but not commanded. In this case Vortigern's question about the dragons unleashes a torrent of eloquence – the 'Prophecies of Merlin', which Geoffrey suspended work on the *History* to write, and then slotted in at this point.

Inspired by the spirit, Merlin starts by answering the king's question. The Red Dragon represents the Britons, the White Dragon represents the Saxons, whom Vortigern has invited into the country. For the moment, the British one (who, by the way, is the ultimate inspiration of the red dragon of Wales) is doomed to defeat. But this is only the beginning. The prophecies take up ten pages of Latin, fourteen in a standard English translation. They fall into two parts, with no visible transition from one to the other.

In the first part, Geoffrey makes Merlin foretell events which, in reality, have already happened. Or, to be more precise, he makes him spin riddles that become increasingly impenetrable; but a few can be seen to fit actual events between the fifth century and the twelfth, and have thus been 'fulfilled'. Anyone who believed that this part of the prophecies was genuinely uttered by Merlin in the fifth century would infer that he did have knowledge of what was, for him, the future. Many medieval readers were credulous enough to think so, and Geoffrey's prestige as Merlin's publicist rose accordingly.

In the first few sentences, which are fairly clear compared with what follows, Merlin continues to talk about the dragons and what they mean. The immediate future, he laments, is dark. The Britons will be overrun, the streams will be red with blood, the churches will be destroyed by the heathen conquerors. But the Red Dragon's recovery portends the rise of a deliverer. First among many characters to be symbolised prophetically by animals, he is 'the Boar of Cornwall'. He will lead resistance, and bring relief from the invaders. This is the first intimation of the coming of Arthur. Merlin predicts that the Boar of Cornwall will rule not only Britain but the islands of the ocean and the forests of Gaul, and he will alarm the Romans. His departure from the scene will be mysterious. He will be immortalised in the Britons' traditions, and his deeds will be nourishment for story-tellers.

Geoffrey is preparing the way for the great king to whom his tale of Merlin is leading up, and whose birth the prophet himself will contrive. He knows the belief that Arthur never died, but lived on in a cave asleep, or in the enchanted isle of Avalon; here, Merlin is foreshadowing that mystery. At this stage of composition, Geoffrey seems to be associating Arthur's end with activities on the continent rather than in Britain. When he actually comes to tell the story, further on, he does introduce continental activities, but opts for a more familiar 'passing of Arthur' back in his own country.

The first batch of pseudo-prophecies wanders on through many obscurities to an allusion to King Henry I, nicknamed 'the Lion of Justice', and to a shipwreck in 1120 in which his son and many companions drowned, 'changed into salt-water fishes'. This tragedy takes the prophecies to their real date of composition soon after the shipwreck, and concludes the first part, though there is nothing in the text to show it. From here onwards, Merlin is being made to foretell things that are in the future for Geoffrey himself. Since he has no way of knowing them, we might expect him to write somewhat less, and to be more cautious in what he says. Not at all. The second part is much longer than the first, and even harder to fit to any credible realities.

The only prediction that makes much sense is an expansion of the old Welsh prophecy of future resurgence that probably initiated the whole exercise:

> The mountains of Armorica shall erupt and Armorica itself shall be crowned with Brutus' diadem. Kambria shall be filled with joy and the Cornish oaks shall flourish. The island shall be called by the name of Brutus and the title given to it by the foreigners shall be done away with.

Brutus, as we saw, is the legendary Trojan founder of the British kingdom, who receives generous coverage in the early chapters of Geoffrey's *History*. Britain, formerly Albion, is said to have been renamed after him. Armorica is the ancient name of the north-west portion of France, which was colonised by Britons and became the Lesser Britain or Brittany, as it still is. The resurgence is to elevate the lands populated by Celtic Britons –

Wales, Cornwall and Brittany too – and the name 'England', Angle-land, is to disappear. This prophecy did achieve a partial fulfilment in 1603 when James Stuart became king of England as well as Scotland, and the inclusive term 'Britain' came back into use – but 'England' was never wholly done away with.

Apart from this, most of Merlin's later prognostications are opaque. A few are topographic. The English Channel is to become so narrow that people will be able to converse across it. Enthusiasts have detected a glimpse of the Channel Tunnel. But an adjacent prophecy is discouraging to would-be literalism: 'The Hedgehog will hide its apples inside Winchester and construct hidden passages under the earth.' This Hedgehog will also build a palace and wall it round with six hundred towers.

As Merlin goes on, he introduces more dragons, a giant or two, and a medley of animals, including a heron, a boar (not the Cornish one), a wolf, a bear, a lion, an ox and an adder. They go through various activities and interactions. Here are some of the most complicated:

> The Fox will come down from the mountains and will metamorphose itself into a Wolf. Under the pretense of holding a conference with the Boar, it will approach that animal craftily and eat it up. Then the Fox will change itself into a Boar and stand waiting for its brothers, pretending that it, too, has lost some of its members. As soon as they come it will kill them with its tusk without a moment's delay and then have itself crowned with a Lion's head.

Some of this imagery might have a meaning in the style of old-fashioned political cartoons, with their British Lion, Russian Bear, and so on. But the reader never gets a key. Eventually, there is a cosmic upheaval, with planets and constellations in disorder. This might be thought to be the end of the world, but apparently it isn't: Merlin's prophecies simply stop, amid floods and storms.

What was Geoffrey doing in this weird farrago, nearly all of which, as an insertion in the *History*, is an irrelevance that slows it down? The answer is that he was doing far more than he intended or realised himself; but what he did intend, and what he did realise, must be considered first.

His most conspicuous addition to the original Dinas Emrys episode is the prophecy of Arthur. Nennius does know of Arthur and has interesting things to say about him, but in other places: his boy-prophet is not said to have foretold him. Geoffrey has Merlin do it, and his Arthurian contribution is larger and subtler than the few sentences about the Boar of Cornwall. He builds up Merlin as a numinous figure, whose anticipation and sponsorship will lend Arthur a more-than-mortal air. The prophecies-after-the-event in the first few pages help to establish his credentials. If he foresaw Henry I, for instance, he must have been an inspired seer.

Geoffrey believes that by writing something very novel and very long, with a few intelligible 'predictions' to give it weight, and dozens of obscure ones to argue over, he can convey the impression that Merlin's words and deeds must be deeply significant. The prophecies are largely mystification, meant to give an impression of profundity. Wace, a poet from Jersey who popularised the *History* in a French paraphrase, left them out because he could not make sense of them. He was not meant to.

Merlin's prophecies have been compared to the notorious quatrains of Nostradamus four centuries later. However, there is no parallel. Nostradamus is cryptic, but in a different way. He is full of circumstantial detail. He gives alleged particulars of people and places and events. His predictions can be nonsense, but enthusiasts claim to find historical fulfilments, and while such claims are nearly all fanciful it is at least possible to make them, in a few cases (a very few) quite plausibly. No amount of enthusiasm could do as well with the prophecies of Merlin.

Nevertheless, some of them *look* as if they ought to mean something, and prophecies-after-the-event which were not recognised as such, like the ones about King Henry, encouraged the illusion. Welshmen, understandably, translated the whole corpus from Geoffrey's Latin. The process did not stop there. French versions were made also, and interpolated in manuscripts of Wace, to fill the gap he had left by not tackling the prophecies himself. When Geoffrey was dead and could no longer be consulted, they were copied and circulated, sometimes with added notes. Commentaries began to appear. One, written about 1170, was attributed (wrongly) to an eminent scholar, Alanus de Insulis. When its author comes to the sentence about Arthur's future vogue among story-tellers, he says: 'Whither has not flying fame spread and familiarised the name of Arthur the Briton, even as far as the empire of Christendom extends?' He says Arthur is renowned not only in western Europe, but in Rome and some Asian countries. The passage may be an exaggeration, but it shows how effective the promotion of Arthur had already become, even in the East, perhaps, through the French-speaking nobility of the Crusader lands. A chronicler not very much later asserts that some Italians put Merlin on a level with Isaiah. There were translations into Dutch and Icelandic, and Spain produced apocryphal prophecies under his name.

This went on for centuries. Merlin's devotees seem to have felt that if they could not grasp what he was talking about, it was probably their own fault rather than his. As late as 1534, the would-be interpretation of Merlin was still so much a recognised activity that Rabelais could make fun of it. In his comic fantasy *Gargantua*, workmen digging foundations for a building find a bronze plate with riddling verses inscribed on it, foretelling a conflict in which violence will be done to the globe. One character works out a religious meaning. Another disagrees: 'The style is like Merlin the Prophet. You can read all the allegorical and serious meanings into it that you like, and dream on about it, you and all the world, as much as ever you will. . . .' His own suggestion is that the verses are about a game of tennis, the globe being the ball which is continually getting hit.

—•— ⚜ —•—

But besides setting the scene for Arthur, and, in doing so, releasing a stream of eccentric speculation, Geoffrey did something far more important. He probably had no notion of what he was doing, but he gave the first impulse to a new way of thinking about the future.

It takes a little reflection to grasp what an innovator he was. Before the twelfth century prophecy by Christians was severely limited in scope. The universal assumption, encouraged by censorious preachers and other disseminators of gloom, was that the world was a fallen place and could never fundamentally change. It would simply drift on till God put an end to it, preferably soon. Christ would return in glory to judge humanity and make all things new, and that was really the only thing to look forward to.

Within that framework of belief, Christian prophecy did occur, but only in relation to the official scheme. Its basis was the last book of the New Testament, the Apocalypse or Revelation of St John, with its spectacular imagery culminating in the end of the world. A few Christians of a literary bent, in the early centuries, dared to enlarge on the Apocalyptist's visions, but still walked in his footsteps. They elaborated his fiery scenario – wars and plagues and tribulations, the Second Coming, divine judgment, the End itself. The more enterprising added characters to the story, including the arch-persecutor Antichrist (whom scripture had hinted at) and a great final earthly ruler, a 'last emperor', who would subdue pagan powers and prepare the way of the Lord.

But these prophets still confined their imaginative flights to the approved theme, the End of the World and its already anticipated prelude in events leading up to it. Apart from these essays in sub-apocalypse, probing of the future was not acceptable as a Christian activity. It was wrong to speculate about other events during the stretch of time between the present day and the beginning of the End. That was the province of soothsayers, sorcerers and kindred practitioners of forbidden arts. They, of course, usually focused on the nearer future, within the prospective lifetime of their dupes, and pretended to tell fortunes. Astrology, which the Greeks and Romans had respected, was a borderline case: after all, the wise men from the East who came to Bethlehem were widely supposed to have been astrologers. But St Augustine, who moulded Christian thinking in this respect as in many others, condemned astrology along with other forms of prognostication. His dismissal was on rational grounds and ably argued. He acknowledged that astrologers' forecasts did sometimes hit the mark, but he said they owed their successes to promptings by evil spirits, who sometimes had knowledge of the future which mortals lacked, and he accused them of leading humanity astray by making it look as if astrology worked.

However, out on the north-west fringes of Christendom, there was one exception to the normal attitude, in the ethnic milieu of Merlin himself. The Christians of Wales were a special case. Their bardic tradition was neither divine nor diabolic. Many were held to have prophetic gifts, and to catch glimpses of the future in undoubted innocence, as when they spoke of their national resurgence or the return of Arthur.

The erudite cleric Gerald of Wales, otherwise Giraldus Cambrensis, defended them ingeniously. He had witnessed Welsh prophesying himself (by seers called *awenyddion*, a term suggesting poetic inspiration), and he believed that they had few counterparts – perhaps none – in other countries. When consulted on some question, they would say a prayer, go into a trance and pour out oracular utterances. These might not seem to be answering the question, but, if you listened carefully, you would find the answer emerging. Afterwards they had to be shaken into wakefulness, and could not remember what they had said, but sometimes retained a vague impression of seeing paper with words written on it.

Yes, said Gerald, perhaps Augustine was right about the evil spirits, but in Wales, perhaps not, or not always. The Welsh, as Geoffrey and earlier authors attested, were of the true British stock descended from the Trojans; and Troy had seers who foresaw the future without using unhallowed magic, and were vindicated by events. Cassandra, for instance, was well known to have prophesied the fall of the city. Merlin belonged to a nation for whom prophesying was ancient, honourable and free from demonic associations. Christians could study him with a clear conscience. Opponents might still argue that even if some of his compatriots were unobjectionable, he was a sorcerer himself, or, if a controlling spirit did speak through him, it was an Augustinian deceiver and should not be listened to. But the fascination of Merlin's prophecies was too powerful, and the impetus towards trust – even uncomprehending trust – too strong.

A new acceptance of such matters was beginning to stir in western Europe. It would be going too far to make Geoffrey responsible for it. But when his *History* became a best-seller, so far as a book ever could before the invention of printing, it played an influential part. Merlin's prophecies encouraged Christians to peer without misgiving into the uncharted time between themselves and the End, and to form ideas about what would happen in it.

Moreover, the ideas could be hopeful. The atmosphere of the late twelfth century was, on the whole, expansive and conducive to thinking about a real change in the world, a change for the better. One major manifestation of this was the birth of a new prophetic doctrine originating with the Italian abbot Joachim of Fiore. He foretold that Christendom would soon enter a new age, the Age of the Holy Spirit. New religious orders, untainted by wealth and power, would lead the way into it. Hierarchies would diminish and be replaced by communities. It would be an era of contemplative wisdom, of peace and love and universal enlightenment. Joachim's teaching was taken up and developed by radical thinkers, and persisted through the Middle Ages in movements of protest and reform. Dante saluted him as a true prophet, and placed him in Heaven among the wisest. A modern historian has described his ideology as the most influential of its kind until the appearance of Marxism.

Joachim and his school of thought made room in the Christian scheme of things for optimism about the earthly future. That was a tremendous and lasting achievement. It went far beyond any influence from Geoffrey's Merlin. Yet to an appreciable extent, it was because of him that it had become permissible to predict anything at any time, without getting preoccupied with the End. To an appreciable extent, it was also because of him that it was becoming legitimate to have earthly hopes.

3

Stonehenge and Tintagel

Geoffrey resumes his *History* when Merlin comes to the end of the prophecies. Vortigern and his attendants are amazed at what they have heard, partly by the sheer strangeness of it, partly by Merlin's self-assurance in speaking freely to the king. But Vortigern is dissatisfied. The young seer has said nothing intelligible about his own fate, and that is what he most wants to hear, even if, as seems likely, it is not reassuring. Merlin is able to summon his controlling spirit again, and this time his prophecy is explicit and alarming. He tells Vortigern to 'run from the fiery vengeance of the sons of Constantine'.

These are the two princes who escaped overseas when Vortigern seized power, and fled to Brittany. The elder is Aurelius Ambrosius. Geoffrey has mentioned him before, but now it is made doubly clear that the 'Ambrosius' at Dinas Emrys was not, as Nennius confusedly thought, the historical British leader Ambrosius Aurelianus. Geoffrey, by a transposition of names, presents this leader as a British prince and rightful heir to the crown. His younger brother is Uther, destined to be known as Uther Pendragon. He is unlikely to be a real historical figure, but he is not a pure invention of Geoffrey's: his name occurs, with the sobriquet, in earlier Welsh poetry. Geoffrey has a story later about a great star, a sort of nova, with a ray ending in a fireball shaped like a dragon;

Merlin associates the portent with Uther, and the style 'Pendragon' is bestowed on him accordingly. Geoffrey says it means 'head of the dragon'. Actually it means 'head dragon' or 'foremost leader'. It is attached almost exclusively to Uther. In one medieval romance Arthur has a brother who is called Pendragon, but Arthur himself never is, and the notion of 'Pendragon' as a title applied to a whole series of British royalties, or to successive custodians of a secret tradition (as in C.S. Lewis's *That Hideous Strength*), is an anachronism.

Uther has not left his mark on the landscape as some of the other characters have. However, there is a small Pendragon Castle in Cumbria, 4 miles south of Kirkby Stephen. The River Eden runs close to it, down in a valley. The ruin stands on an artificial mound and dates to the late twelfth century. Those who take the name seriously suggest that there was a previous fortification on the site, built for Uther. The place does have a legend about him, that he tried unsuccessfully to divert the river and make a moat. According to a local rhyme:

> Let Uther Pendragon do what he can,
> Eden will run where Eden ran.

To revert to Merlin's warning to Vortigern, there is more of it. Geoffrey says he went on to announce that the threat from Constantine's sons was immediate:

> At this very moment they are fitting out their ships. Even as I speak they are leaving the coasts of Armorica and spreading their sails to cross the sea. They will make for the island of Britain, attack the Saxon people and conquer the race which they detest.

Merlin saw two possibilities for Vortigern, neither of them welcome. His Saxon allies would kill him, or the returning princes would do the same, to avenge the death of their father. Merlin looked beyond. Aurelius and Uther would both reign, but their lives would be cut short. Vortigern's family would have a hand in some further trouble-making, but the Boar of Cornwall (here again is Geoffrey's prophetic term for Arthur) would 'eat them up'. Merlin was looking decades ahead, since the Boar of Cornwall was not yet born.

Aurelius and his brother landed at Totnes in Devon, like Brutus the Trojan long before, as well as several other characters in the *History*. The reason for Geoffrey's interest in this port is not apparent; he may see it as simply a place of good omen, because of the original Trojan arrival. As news of the princes' landing spread, the Britons, who had been scattered far and wide by the Saxon onslaughts, came together again with revived optimism. As quickly as possible, the appropriate clergy were convened and crowned Aurelius king, anointing him and doing homage according to the forms prescribed. The British leaders clamoured for an offensive against the Saxons. Aurelius's passionate desire for revenge against the betrayer of his father and elder brother caused him to give priority to the hunting down of Vortigern, but he was appalled to see the ruin which the usurper's pro-Saxon policy had brought on Britain, and he agreed to take action against the heathen directly after.

Merlin's words at Dinas Emrys caused Vortigern to leave the scene precipitately. He headed for a stronghold on a hill called Cloartius, at Genoreu. Over-critical readers have seen an inconsistency here, since his place of refuge was always previously said to be in Snowdonia, but as his tower was never built, Geoffrey is consistent in taking him to a bolt-hole somewhere else.

His flight can be traced. Genoreu is Ganarew, a couple of miles from Geoffrey's native Monmouth along the road to Ross-on-Wye, and close to the fringes of the Forest of Dean. Cloartius is the hill of Little Doward (properly Doartius, mis-spelt by a copyist). It has an Iron Age fort, and, here as elsewhere, fifth-century timber structures may have been built inside. Geoffrey may have picked this hill simply because it was near his home and he was familiar with it. However, the area does have legendary associations. In the hillside, set back among trees, is 'Arthur's Cave' – one of several in various parts of Britain. This has traces of occupation in the Stone Age, and perhaps also in late Roman times, more or less when Geoffrey brings Vortigern to the neighbourhood. It differs from most of England's 'Arthur's Caves' because it is real and accessible. Nearly all the others are elusive places where Arthur is supposed to lie in enchanted sleep.

Geoffrey notes that 'Genoreu' is in the district of Erging, a name derived from Ariconium, the name of a Roman settlement east of Ross-on-Wye. Erging covered a large area, and was later called Archenfield. Here Nennius, or some other contributor to his book, speaks of the burial mound of Amr, a son of Arthur. Arthur himself killed his son in some grim and unrecorded dispute. The mound may have been Wormelow Tump near the source of the Gamber, once a well-known landmark, but this no longer exists. Vortigern occupied his hilltop before Aurelius located him, but when Aurelius caught up, he moved promptly to destroy the usurper. His soldiers had difficulty breaking into the fort, but they set fire to it – a real possibility with a fifth-century building – and Vortigern perished in the flames, as Merlin had predicted. He had lost whatever popular backing he ever had, and the brothers pressed on without meeting any resistance from their compatriots.

News of this catastrophe alarmed Hengist and the Saxons with him. He knew that Aurelius was not only an inspired leader but a skilful and powerful individual fighter, on foot and on horseback, and that his general conduct was making him popular. Hengist brought together a force of picked men and tried to convince them that there was no need to be afraid of the Britons. Two fierce battles ensued, and the Saxons might have won if it had not been for the arrival of Breton cavalry. As it turned out, Hengist was captured, dragged into the British ranks and beheaded. His execution at last ended his depredations in Britain. Immediately afterwards, Aurelius led his army to York and received the surrender of Hengist's son Octa. An agreement was reached allowing Saxon settlement in the less populous parts of Britain.

After Aurelius had done what he could to repair the damage to the kingdom, he made a personal pilgrimage to the mass grave of the British nobles slaughtered by Hengist. He undertook it at the suggestion of a bishop, Eldadus, who himself had founded the cemetery to house the bodies after the massacre. At that time Eldadus had been a monk at the monastery of Amesbury. Geoffrey's description of the locality is confused, but he has a notion of elevated ground somewhere not far from the monastery, which he would have known about, because the monastery was famous in Welsh tradition for a 'perpetual choir', with monks chanting the divine office in relays around the clock. This is all vague, but there is nothing vague about his account of the royal visit and its result.

Aurelius inspected the cemetery and wept, seeing only a meaningless expanse of grass, with nothing commemorating the victims. He decided to set up a memorial on the site, and formed a committee, with predictable results. It put him in much the same position as Prince Albert in a later age, confronted, as chairman of the committee for the Great Exhibition, with conflicting plans for housing it. Aurelius assembled stonemasons, carpenters and other craftsmen from all over Britain, but they had the same sort of difficulty in agreeing on a plan. Their report was discouraging.

Then Tremorinus, the Archbishop of Caerleon, put a suggestion to the king that broke the deadlock: 'If there is anyone anywhere who has the ability to execute your plan, then Merlin, the prophet of Vortigern, is the man to do it. In my opinion, there is no one else in your kingdom who has greater skill, either in the foretelling of the future or in mechanical contrivances.' This is very peculiar indeed. To begin with, Geoffrey assumes that Merlin was now an adult, after only a brief interval. Perhaps his paternity caused him to mature unusually fast. But that is only the beginning. Why does the archbishop think of Merlin at all? He could have been remembered only as a young visionary in a remote part of Wales. Aurelius would have heard about Vortigern's panic-stricken flight, but might well have been uninformed as to the motive for it. Neither he nor anyone at his court went to Dinas Emrys, or sought out its occupant.

Yet Tremorinus, whose see is nowhere near the place, knows of Merlin and has a soaring opinion of his abilities. Up to now, Merlin has never been anything but a prophet. The archbishop knows him as such, but also as someone with an entirely different gift, which has never been hinted at before. Merlin is still a prophet, but he is also an architect and an engineer. There is nothing to show when or how he acquired his expertise, or where he displayed it. Yet his reputation has reached the archbishop. Without preparation, Geoffrey is adding a new dimension to the character. And it is not a magical dimension, as, looking back in a literary retrospect, we might suppose. Merlin has not been portrayed as a wizard in the first part of his career, and he is still not portrayed as a wizard in the second. He is a man of eminently practical talents, which are raised, as soon appears, to a superhuman power, completely without explanation. Tremorinus knows him in both capacities, the prophetic and the practical, and keeps them distinct with no magical fudge.

Geoffrey tells how Aurelius 'asked many questions about Merlin', clearly having no information. Satisfied, he sent messengers about the country to find him and escort him back, in a repetition of Vortigern's search, though this time with no sinister intention. Again the search was extensive. At last the messengers traced him in the territory of the Gewissei – Gwent, in south-east Wales – which had once been Vortigern's domain; seemingly, Merlin had explored it himself after his dismissal of the usurper, and had taken a liking to the Galabes Springs, where the messengers found him.

They conducted him to Aurelius, who was delighted to meet him, but got off on the wrong foot. He still thought of his guest primarily as a prophet, and ordered him to foretell something. Merlin, for the moment, had shed his prophetic function. He was not overawed by the situation, and replied with a firm and significant negative: 'Mysteries of that sort cannot be revealed except when there is the most urgent need for them. If I were to utter them as an entertainment, or where there was no need at all, then the spirit which controls me would forsake me in the moment of need.' Here is his spirit again, still unnamed and undefined, but dominant.

Others at the court made the same request, and received the same refusal. But it was a different story when they turned to the matter in hand. The king gave up on prophecy and explained his plan for a monument. Merlin replied without hesitation, not even discussing the pros and cons of the case or consulting the royal counsellers. He told Aurelius to bring over the Giants' Ring from Ireland. The Giants' Ring (or Round-Dance — Chorea) was on Mount Killaraus (possibly Kildare). It was a colossal circle of standing stones such as no man living could shift or raise, unless, perhaps, he had exceptional skill. If Aurelius had them taken down, shipped to Britain, and arranged in position around the burial site, precisely as in Ireland, nothing could ever shake them.

Aurelius laughed. If the stones were as enormous and heavy as Merlin said, how could they be uprooted and carried so far? And what was the point? Britain had plenty of big stones of its own. Why not simply build a circle with home-grown materials? It would be just as good.

Merlin advised the king to take his proposition seriously. The circle that he spoke of was not a collection of rocks such as you might find anywhere. It was a focus of special energies, spiritual and physical. A very long time ago, when giants lived in Ireland and parts of Africa, some of them assembled these stones in Africa and transported them to Ireland, where they set them up on Mount Killaraus. All the stones had medicinal properties. If a sick person was placed in a bath at the foot of one of them, water that was poured over the stone and ran down into the bath could effect a cure. The giants mixed the water with herbal infusions, and applied the liquid to wounds for healing. The Giants' Ring was a temple of life.

This is a curious touch. It does not seem to fit in with any known legend. Has Merlin simply made it up – or at any rate, improved some dubious rumour – as a clinching argument? The natural objection is that he would be discredited when the stones were in Britain and didn't heal anyone. However, they would probably not be put to the test. Once they were in position as guardians of the royal cemetery, sick people would never be allowed to enter the hallowed precinct and sit in baths there.

The Britons, however wishfully, were convinced. They vowed to get the stones, even if the Irish resisted and had to be fought. The king's brother Uther sailed over with an army, taking Merlin as consultant. Gillomanius, the Irish king, was amused. The Britons were fools, and it was understandable that the Saxons had had the upper hand for so long. He echoed Aurelius's first comment: Why weren't British stones good enough? Why go to all the trouble to steal Irish ones? Apparently he knew nothing of their alleged healing properties. He tried but failed to stop Uther with his own army, and the Britons reached the Giants' Ring.

They were awestruck. Merlin addressed them: 'Try your strength, young men, and see whether skill can do more than brute strength, or strength more than skill, when it comes to dismantling these stones!' They brought up ladders and ropes and other apparatus, but could not budge the stones. Then Merlin came forward. He placed apparatus of his own in position, and lowered the circle with no trouble at all. Thus, he showed that artistry was better than brute strength.

What is a reader meant to think at this point? The story may look like the beginning of Merlin's transformation into a magician. Yet all the emphasis is on skill and general know-how. There is no clue to what he actually did. A twelfth-century author, however imaginative, would never have thought of power-driven machinery.

The job was not finished. Under Merlin's direction, the stones were loaded on to ships, and a fair wind carried the fleet back to Britain. Uther's host disembarked and set off across country with the stones. Geoffrey gives no hint as to how they were transported on land. Possibly the soldiers trundled them along on rollers, or perhaps Merlin used his arts again, in some other way. However it was done, the custodians of the Ring kept moving.

As soon as Aurelius heard, he sent out heralds all over the kingdom summoning his people to the burial site. For some, the journey was a long one. But clergy and laity responded with enthusiasm. In the presence of a large assembly, Aurelius took up a crown and placed it on his own head. The time was Pentecost, and he presided over a three-day festival. It was not all holiday: having so many of his subjects together, he took the opportunity to attend to administrative matters. Several men presented themselves who had supported him loyally through difficult times, and he rewarded them with grants of land. He also appointed new bishops for sees that had fallen vacant. By the time the more immediate steps had been taken, the great stones from Ireland had arrived, and were ready to be raised into position. The king ordered Merlin to stand them in a circle around the cemetery. Merlin did so. He had evidently drawn a plan and taken measurements, as he exactly reproduced the original formation – a further proof that skill was better than strength alone. The reconstituted Ring was so secure that it stands to this day.

Yes, we are on Salisbury Plain, and it's Stonehenge that we are talking about! Geoffrey doesn't call it Stonehenge till later, when he is telling his readers its English name. But the episode is clear, and this is the earliest known reference to the monument. Incidentally, a manuscript illustration of Merlin at work is the earliest known picture. Since Stonehenge has been in place for thousands of years, Geoffrey's fifth-century project might be dismissed as fantasy in a void, though he connects it with later parts of the *History* by saying that three kings – Aurelius himself, Uther, and another Constantine, Arthur's successor – were all buried inside the Ring. But apart from such would-be verisimilitude, he does really know something about Stonehenge; and a careful consideration of the great megalith may bring this into view, and shed light on both the author and his astonishing creation.

❖

Geoffrey, almost certainly, has no first-hand knowledge of Stonehenge. For one thing, he is confused about the geography; for another, he simplifies the Ring itself. It is actually a composite – or, at least, what is left of a composite – structure, created over a long stretch of time, and it is far more complicated than Geoffrey imagines. Its English name is related to the Anglo-Saxon word *hengen*, 'hanging'. It was used to mean a gibbet, and may have been applied in this case because the cross-pieces or lintels on top of the uprights suggested enormous gibbets. But the idea may have been simply that the cross-pieces were supposed to have been 'hung' there, in some unspecified way.

Salisbury Plain was once Britain's principal centre of population, with numerous trackways converging on it. One

43

sign of its ancient importance is the number of burial mounds. While megaliths are numerous in the British Isles and beyond, the huge main circle of Stonehenge, Geoffrey's Ring, is unparalleled, not only because of its architectural effect but because the great stones have been artificially smoothed and shaped, a very slow, laborious process with the tools that were available. The contrast with Avebury is glaring. The actual area of Avebury is much larger – it has a whole village inside it – and the stones are big and impressive, but they are not shaped and they are not connected.

Stonehenge began as a circular enclosure about 300 feet across. The boundary was a bank of chalk rubble, which is still there, though not as high as it used to be. Just inside the perimeter there were fifty-six pits, now called Aubrey Holes after John Aubrey, the man who discovered them in the seventeenth century. Some, when excavated, were found to contain cremated human bones, which may or may not have been the remains of sacrifices. For centuries this enclosure made up the whole of Stonehenge. Then the chiefs, or priests, or whoever controlled the site, had two stone circles built inside it. The components were geologically bluestones, quite small compared with those that came after. They were presently taken down and replaced by the huge structure known to Geoffrey, his Giants' Ring, much of which is still standing, and constitutes the familiar spectacle seen from a distance.

The great uprights are called sarsen stones. The word seems to be derived from 'Saracen', for no obvious reason. Weighing between 25 and 50 tons, they are blocks of extremely hard sandstone, quarried 20 miles away on the Marlborough Downs, and moved slowly across the country on rollers or sledges dragged by human teams; there does not seem to be any evidence for oxen or other draught animals. The possibility of this long haul has been proved by experiments with volunteers. To modern sceptics, puzzled by ancient feats such as this, the main answer is that time was emphatically not of the essence. The work was performed a little at a time, and spread over decades, even centuries.

Assembled on the site, the stones were manoeuvred into a vertical position. The cross-pieces, weighing about 7 tons, were laid on top, with sockets on the underside fitting over knobs on the uprights, together forming trilithons. The techniques used by Merlin and by the real builders are not on record, and various suggestions have been put forward. The uprights may have been toppled into pits, with the earth afterwards dug away to leave them standing with a fallacious air of having been hoisted into position. The lintels were arranged with great skill to bridge the gaps. There have been theories about long ramps with a very gradual incline.

In a final phase, some of the discarded bluestones were brought back inside. A stone lying on the ground, nicknamed the 'altar stone', may be only a fallen pillar. The implication of human sacrifice is a by-product of the theory that Stonehenge was a Druid temple – a theory best deferred for the moment. Stonehenge, even the last-built part of it, is older than the Druids.

The actual age of the main circle has been subject to re-thinking. It used to be dated to 1600–1500 BC. Advocates of this dating, such as R.J.C. Atkinson, argued that it was designed by someone familiar with Mycenae in Greece – a notion supportive of a kind of inverted colonialist attitude that was once the norm: that practically all western civilisation came from Greece, and that the Neolithic inhabitants of Britain were barbarians, even savages, who could invent nothing themselves. However, a recalibration of the carbon-dating by Colin Renfrew pushed the circle back to a time before 2000 BC, when influence from Mycenae was out of the question. The estimate of the indigenous people's abilities is correspondingly higher than it was.

What was Stonehenge for? It hardly looks residential. Somebody once suggested, I believe seriously, that in the fifth century it had a canopy over the top and looked from a distance like an immense table – hence, King Arthur's Round Table! Even if this were so, it would not explain the original function, in an age long before Arthur. It is generally interpreted as a temple, though not a Druid one. Positive evidence is scanty. The system appears to be oriented towards the place where the sun rises at the summer solstice, and sun-worship is a natural inference, but in the absence of written records the nature of the in-dwelling deity is unknown. Wiltshire and neighbouring areas, in the third millennium BC, had the population and the potential for the unique task of creating Stonehenge, and it may have been a kind of sacred capital for a large part of Britain, but nothing emerges as to what happened there. Attempts have been made to link it with timber structures inferred at Woodhenge, a couple of miles away, in a ritual relationship.

There are various related legends and superstitions. According to a long-established belief, which is part of the ineffaceable sense of mystery, the stones cannot be counted. Sir Philip Sidney mentions this in a poem. John Evelyn the diarist and Jonathan Swift both attempted the count with different results. Daniel Defoe has a tale about a baker who brought a cartload of loaves, and placed a loaf on each stone as he counted it. However, he checked his figures by repeating the count more than once, and kept getting a different answer. H.G. Wells mentions the reputed impossibility in a short story, *The Door in the Wall*. Most of the early reckoners arrived at a figure in the low nineties. They were not far wrong; the discrepancies were due mainly to uncertainty over what to count as a stone.

— ✦ ⚔ ✦ —

In studying Stonehenge's alleged transplantation, and the inferences about Geoffrey of Monmouth and Merlin, it is important to understand that the account in the *History* is the only one that is authentically Geoffrey's.

There is a serio-comic alternative in which Merlin subcontracts the job. The Devil takes it on, and handles it with great ingenuity. At that time (presumably in the fifth century) the land in Ireland where the stone circle stood belonged to an old woman who had no particular reverence for it, and had enclosed it in her extensive garden. The Devil visited her in a respectable guise that inspired confidence, and explained that he wanted the stones and would pay for them. He poured out a heap of coins. They were of outlandish denominations — four-and-a-half pence, nine pence, thirteen pence — but the old woman showed remarkable trust. The Devil promised that she could keep as much money as she could count while he removed the stones. She agreed to the bargain, assuming that the operation would take a long time and enable her to do well out of it. However, the Devil quickly uprooted the stones, bound them in a willow withy and flew to Salisbury Plain carrying the bundle. Merlin received it intact, except for a single stone that had worked loose and fallen into the Avon near Bulford, presumably while the Devil was circling to land. I have seen this tale, or something like it, quoted as an authentic version of Geoffrey's story. I have even seen it quoted as the only one. But Geoffrey had nothing to do with it. Large-scale magic and diabolic agency were foreign to his imagination. The trick played on the woman and the flight from Ireland to Salisbury Plain were invented by the antiquary John Wood in the eighteenth century.

The first fact to emphasise, if it needs emphasising, is that while Geoffrey invites us to think that the monument has only been on Salisbury Plain since the fifth century, he doesn't pretend that it began there or that Merlin conjured it into existence on the spot. In later literature King Arthur's capital, Camelot, does occasionally seem to have sprung from nowhere, perhaps even under Merlin's auspices. That is not the case with the Giants' Ring. Geoffrey is quite clear that it is very old indeed, but not as a feature of the plain. Its history began somewhere else, namely in Ireland. And its builders were giants.

Who were they? About giants in general, different mythologies have different things to say, and some are irrelevant. We must distinguish. In ancient Greece the giants are the offspring of Heaven and Earth, but not the first such offspring. Before them came the senior deities called Titans. Their leader Cronus had a son, Zeus, who led a successful revolt against his father and became ruler of the universe, heading the company of Olympian gods, his siblings. Zeus banished the Titans to distant places, some of them to a subterranean prison, while Cronus himself was sent to an island over the Atlantic, where he lies asleep. Another Titan, Prometheus, broke ranks and aided Zeus in his revolt, but then fell out with him over the recently created human species. Zeus had a poor opinion of humans and wanted to abolish them. Prometheus befriended them and stole fire from heaven for their use. For this pro-human deed and others, Zeus banished Prometheus to a mountain in the Caucasus, where he was chained to a rock with a vulture periodically gnawing his vitals.

Heaven and Earth generated a second brood, and these were the original giants of Greek mythology. They were monstrous creatures, some of whom had a semi-human form, but none of them was human or, like Prometheus, friendly to humanity. They revolted against the gods and, among other feats, piled a mountain on top of another mountain – Pelion on Ossa – in a bid to scale Olympus. Zeus defeated and dispersed them, though some were allowed to live on unobtrusively. In Sicily, for instance, several one-eyed Cyclopses led a pastoral existence. The most famous was Polyphemus, who ate several of Odysseus's crew and had his one eye put out by the vengeful Greeks.

These Earth-born giants, however, had no place in the mythology of the British Isles, and they were not the species that Geoffrey had in mind when he explained the origin of Stonehenge. The same applies to the Scandinavian giants, who lived in Jotunheim and embodied primordial powers of chaos. The Norse gods, led by Odin, struggled against them to establish cosmic order. Mortals were the gods' allies in the struggle. But, again, they are irrelevant.

Geoffrey, through Merlin, is evoking giants of legend and folklore who were far closer to humanity – who, in fact, were magnified human beings, in a more or less historical context. Traditions of giants like these were not very widespread. One reason for belief in them was that bones of large animals, unearthed accidentally or deliberately, were taken for the bones of large men. More important, and more relevant to Stonehenge, was a human propensity for guesswork about impressive ruins and other structures that were recognised as the work of an earlier generation. It was assumed that the earlier generation must have been very large and strong, because contemporaries would not have been equal to the task. This fancy, resulting from an undervaluation of the contemporaries, was never universal. Plenty of travellers saw the Egyptian pyramids without jumping to conclusions about pre-dynastic Egyptian colossi. When the fancy did occur, it sometimes singled out one person, a hero with more than mortal powers: in Ireland, for example, Finn MacCool was credited with building the Giant's Causeway, among other feats. But the motif of magnified humans as a long-ago race had attraction for anyone who reflected on megaliths, of which Stonehenge itself was the outstanding example.

A loose network of megalithic cultures spread over the central Mediterranean and parts of western Europe, including the British Isles, from the fourth millennium BC. Sometimes the handlers of the great stones built what appear to have been temples, as in Malta. Sometimes they made circles and linear patterns, as in Brittany and Cornwall. Sometimes they put up individual stones. No one knows why, though there are features, such as the solar alignment at Stonehenge, which suggest astronomical interests. Theorists have detected cultic linkages, with adherents of a megalithic religion spreading it across western Europe. It may be so, but there are no direct proofs.

Geoffrey, however, does transmit a notion about giant builders, whatever their purpose may have been. In Britain this is rather uncommon: where folklore has anything to say about the great stones, it is apt to assert that they are people turned to stone as punishment for their sins, such as dancing on Sunday. By connecting them with giants, associated with Africa and the British Isles, Geoffrey is setting aside popular lore, and showing awareness of the actual megalithic spread.

Again, who were his giants, and where did they come from? Medieval minds harboured ideas about a giant race, quite apart from any megalithic mythology. Biblical commitments, however, imposed restrictions. Scripture did mention such a race in a primordial world – 'there were giants in those days' – but since the Flood any humans anywhere, even enlarged ones, must have originated after it because it drowned everybody except the family of Noah, whose sons Shem, Ham and Japheth became universal patriarchs. The Bible dated the Flood around the middle of the third millennium BC, so the giants, and anything that they built, must have appeared later. Moreover, since all the peoples of the world were descended from Shem, Ham and Japheth, every nation had to be traceable to one of the three. Genesis chapter 10 makes an attempt – a thoughtful and well-informed attempt, for its period – to do this. Shem was the ancestor of the Hebrews and other 'Semites' (this is where the word came from). Japheth was the ancestor of the more or less respectable Greeks and other Europeans. That left Ham, who had a bad reputation and whose progeny were under a cloud. Medieval writers classified the giants among the descendants of Ham. It is not clear why any descendants of a normal-sized son of Noah should have grown enormous. However it happened, some migrated from Africa about 1700 BC and settled in the British Isles. Among them were the giants whom Geoffrey describes as bringing over the stones of the Giants' Ring. The implied date for it is closer to Atkinson's than to Renfrew's, but is not utterly ridiculous.

Giants inhabited Britain, then called Albion, for about six hundred years. In Geoffrey's *History*, their dominance ends with the arrival of the Trojan proto-Britons, about 1100 BC. By that time their numbers had declined steeply and only a few were left. According to Geoffrey they were concentrated in Cornwall, an idea inspired by the many standing stones in that county, which suggested a lingering but diminishing presence. The Trojans, as we saw, wiped them out.

How big were these giants? Big enough to transport megaliths thousands of miles over land and water, and set them up at the end of their journey – an operation which, according to Geoffrey, was impossible for normal-sized people, and required the techniques of Merlin. Yet Geoffrey is inconsistent. He informs his readers that one of the Cornish remnant was 12 cubits tall: say 18 feet. Yet he seems to forget this measurement a moment later when he describes a wrestling match in which Corineus, the Trojan after whom Cornwall was named, not only defeated the giant but carried him uphill on his shoulders and tossed him into the sea.

Traditions of Cornish giants survived for centuries after Geoffrey. They were no longer thought of as forming a tribe or community; they became isolated figures, rather stupid, and given to aimless fighting with boulders. One was Cormoran, who lived in a forest that formerly covered the floor of Mount's Bay (this forest, by the way, did exist). He and his wife collected lumps of white granite to build a stronghold, St Michael's Mount. Cormoran was slain by Jack the Giant-Killer. Another was Bolster, who made an attempt on the virtue of St Agnes, but was outwitted. Geoffrey's vacillation about the giants' size continued to be reflected. Bolster was huge out of all proportion to ordinary mortals. He could stand with one foot on Carn Brea and the other on St Agnes Beacon, 6 miles apart. Yet his proposition to Agnes implies that their dimensions were not so immensely different. The fact is that imaginary giants everywhere seem to have a certain elasticity. Rabelais's Gargantua begins by being enormous, yet later in the story he can sit in an ordinary chair. Paul Bunyan, the American super-lumberjack, grows bigger and bigger as his saga drifts westward, till he is creating natural features such as the Grand Canyon. Geoffrey himself, by the way, has a couple of isolated giants, though not in Cornwall. One is Retho in Snowdonia, the other lives on Mont-Saint-Michel in Normandy. Both are violent and repellent.

The hints that he had some awareness of megalithic antiquity become more specific when the focus shifts from Stonehenge's sarsens to the smaller bluestones that preceded them on the site. Geology shows that they were not local – not even, like the sarsens, fairly local. For unknown magical or ritual reasons, they were quarried in the Prescelly Mountains in south-west Wales and conveyed from there to Salisbury Plain. With whatever difficulty, they could have been transported on rafts up the Bristol Channel, and then perhaps up the Bristol Avon. This reconstruction has been disputed, on the grounds that the bluestones might be natural blocks that were carried along from the Prescelly Mountains by glacial action. But it seems odd that the ice should have obligingly set them down in a cluster in such a convenient place, and Renfrew and other authorities accept human agency. Geoffrey's story of components of Stonehenge being brought by sea from Ireland is not the same as a story of components of Stonehenge being brought by sea from Wales, but a sea-borne journey from the west would be such an unlikely thing to invent that a tradition of the Prescelly operation, handed down as part of some ancient saga, cannot be ruled out. On this topic, there will be more to come, with an illumination of Merlin.

To revert to the *History* . . . The great ceremony at the royal burial site did not bring peace. Vortigern's son Paschent was ambitious to avenge his father and regain the power his father had held. Understandably having few British supporters, he tried to enlist foreign aid, but King Aurelius routed a contingent of German mercenaries. Paschent turned to Ireland and won over King Gillomanius, who was annoyed at the seizure of the Giants' Ring by Vortigern's enemies. The allies landed near St David's in Wales. Aurelius was lying ill at Winchester, and his brother Uther led a British force against the invasion.

Paschent, who had learned nothing from his father's experience, was busy recruiting Saxons. One of them, Eopa, approached him with an offer to assassinate the king if he were paid enough. Paschent accepted. Eopa could speak the British language and had some medical skill. Posing as a doctor, he made his way to Winchester and poisoned Aurelius, who died in his sleep. The news was slow in reaching Uther, who was trying to find the enemy in Wales.

It was at this time that the celestial portent appeared that gave him his sobriquet 'Pendragon'. A brilliant new star blazed in the sky, with a single beam shining from it, which ended in a small fiery cloud shaped like a dragon. Two rays of light issuing from the dragon's mouth seemed to point towards Gaul and the Irish Sea. The portent appeared on three successive nights and spread consternation among the Britons. Uther was alarmed himself, and summoned his wise men.

Among them was Merlin, who had accompanied the army as an adviser. He took centre stage immediately at the consultation, summoned his spirit of prophecy, and wept. He knew, as no one else did, that Aurelius was dead, and hence his grief. But he saluted Uther as the new king and urged him to act at once to secure his position. The star with its attendant dragon designated Uther himself. The rays of light signified his two children, not yet born: a son who would be a great leader and conqueror, and a daughter whose descendants would be rulers of Britain.

Uther had his doubts, but he pressed on towards the enemy camp near St David's. Paschent marched out with his Irish and Saxon allies. Uther won a hotly contested battle. Paschent and Gillomanius were both killed, and the invaders fled, with the angry local inhabitants in pursuit. Uther hurried to Winchester, where his brother's death was confirmed. Aurelius was buried inside the Giants' Ring, and Uther was unanimously accepted as his successor. As a permanent memento of Merlin's revelation, he had two golden dragons made, like the dragon that had appeared in the sky. He presented one to Winchester Cathedral and kept the other for himself, as a mascot to carry with him on future campaigns.

Its magical protection, if any, was needed. The Saxons in Britain had still not given up. Hengist's son Octa, with a kinsman named Eosa, denounced the agreement that had been made with Aurelius. He gathered together all the Saxons and Germans who had fought for the late Paschent, and ravaged the north. He besieged York. Uther tried to raise the siege and was repulsed with heavy losses. For a moment, it looked as if Hengist's power in Britain might be restored by his son. Uther's weakened army took refuge on a wooded hill. Having no notion how to cope with defeat, he asked his chief officers for suggestions, and paid special attention to Gorlois, the Duke of Cornwall, 'a man of great experience and mature years'. Uther was still young, probably not out of his twenties. Gorlois persuaded him to take the more numerous enemy by surprise in a night attack. This was successful, and the Saxons were routed. Octa and Eosa were taken prisoner. Gorlois had rescued his inexperienced chief and saved the kingdom from the threatened Saxon recovery. Uther, as would soon be apparent, had a curious way of showing gratitude.

He led his army into the turbulent north on a mission of pacification, and occupied the fortified town of Alclud or Alcluith, 'Rock of Clyde', better known since as Dumbarton, a Gaelic-derived name meaning 'Fort of the Britons'. An earlier chapter of Geoffrey's *History* informs the reader that it was founded about 1000 BC by a British king, Ebraucus, who also founded York, and had twenty wives by whom he had twenty sons and thirty daughters. Geoffrey meticulously names them all. While he was inaccurate about Ebraucus, he was right in thinking that Alclud had existed for a long time.

Its fort is on a headland formed by a bare volcanic mass of basalt, 240 feet high, jutting into the Clyde. This is the Rock. Excavation has shown that the place was important in the fifth century, perhaps as a centre of government, so it was plausible to claim that Uther made it his northern headquarters. Later it became the capital of the north British kingdom of Strathclyde.

A local legend declares that the Rock only came to be where it is because of St Patrick, who was living near Glasgow before his Irish enterprise. The Devil scented danger and assembled a horde of witches, who pursued Patrick down the river. He leaped into a boat and pushed off, knowing that the witches would not be able to cross running water. They tore up part of a hill and threw it after him, but it fell short and is now the Rock.

Geoffrey knows nothing of this tale, and it is not in his style. Like Stonehenge's apocryphal flight, the episode underlines a crucial distinction. Geoffrey has a down-to-earth quality. He may adopt far-fetched motifs like the concealment of the dragons at Dinas Emrys, but he never invents spectacular feats of magic. His restraint in this respect needs to be borne in mind when interpreting Merlin's final performance in the *History*.

Starting from his base at Dumbarton, Uther made a tour of Scotland. Strictly speaking, Geoffrey misuses the name; Caledonia was not yet the domain of the Scots. They began its conquest afterwards, and the northerners whom Uther dealt with would have been Picts. Whatever they should be called, Geoffrey regards their country at that time as 'a land frightful to live in', a lurking-place for Picts, Scots and other savages, and a refuge for Saxons too. Uther 'reclaimed its rebellious people from their state of savagery' and established law and order as his predecessors had never entirely managed to do. Returning to London with the defeated Saxon leaders, he had them imprisoned.

Geoffrey is now approaching the event that he has been building up to ever since Merlin's first manifestation. He has set the stage with the destruction of enemies and the unification of Britain, and Arthur, his climactic hero, is now to be ushered on to the stage. Merlin has prophesied Arthur twice, in cryptic language. Now the prophet will act himself. Yet the action he takes will have a mystery of its own.

Here is the story of Arthur's origin. At Easter, after his pacification of the north, Uther held a celebratory festival in London. All his nobles attended. Among them was the Duke of Cornwall, the same loyal follower who had recently saved him from defeat. Gorlois was no longer young, but he brought his young wife Ygerna, who was considered to be the most beautiful woman in Britain. As soon as Uther saw her he was totally smitten, and gave her all his attention. He kept ordering dishes of food to be passed to her, and sent servants with golden goblets of wine, continually smiling and 'engaging her in sprightly conversation'. Her husband judged that the conversation was becoming too sprightly, but he could hardly protest in public. Instead, he left the court without asking the king's permission, taking Ygerna with him.

Uther, already in the wrong, seized on this lack of courtesy to put himself further in the wrong. He ordered Gorlois to come back. When he refused, Uther, regardless of the duke's past services to him, assembled his troops and marched down to Cornwall, where he inflicted senseless damage wherever he went. Gorlois gathered his own outnumbered retainers in a fortified place called Dimilioc, possibly the prehistoric encampment known as Tregeare Rounds, 5 miles from his castle at Tintagel. The king promptly besieged him.

Meanwhile, not caring to keep Ygerna with him in such a dangerous situation, and afraid that Uther would find and kidnap her, Gorlois had immured her in Tintagel Castle itself, believing that even the royal army could not force a way in. It was a reasonable belief. There was no easy approach. That is still more or less true. From the village a ravine runs down to a cove between two dramatic headlands, looking out directly across the Atlantic. Today, a path on the left divides, one branch descending to the beach, the other leading upwards to the headland on that side.

The headland, a mass of rock towering above the ocean, is nearly an island. Its only link with the mainland is a ridge that has crumbled, leaving a chasm. The path crosses a bridge over the chasm to a steep flight of steps, ascending to the remains of the castle. These date from the thirteenth century, after Geoffrey, who could not have known of the castle when he wrote his *History*, because it was not there; but he evidently did know of a much older settlement, higher up on the promontory, and that was what he made out to have been Gorlois's stronghold.

Tintagel is of historic importance because it was here that Ralegh Radford discovered high-quality imported pottery that could be dated to the fifth and sixth centuries; when found on other sites, this supplied an archaeological key to the 'Arthurian' period. Tintagel's function is still open to debate, but it was very probably a regional centre of government, and a credible residence, at least in the milder parts of the year, for Gorlois and his wife.

The siege of Dimilioc had been going on for a week, but Uther was still brooding over Ygerna. His desire for her, even in her absence, was growing ungovernable. He confessed it to a friend, Ulfin, talking like some nineteenth-century romantic about dying if he couldn't have her, and asking, as on other occasions, for advice. Ulfin remarked that the ridge connecting the castle with the mainland was so narrow that three armed guards (like Macaulay's Horatius and his comrades keeping the bridge) could prevent anyone from getting across. However, Ulfin had a constructive suggestion: send for Merlin.

Merlin was sent for. He was with the besieging army and arrived at once. He realised that the state Uther was in was no ordinary passion, and would need to be dealt with by an unprecedented measure. He had 'drugs' that would change the king's appearance and make him look exactly like Gorlois, so as to deceive the guards and, after that, Ygerna herself. If Uther agreed to try them, they could be used to disguise Ulfin and Merlin also. Uther followed Merlin's instructions, and the three, their appearance transformed, came to the castle as night was falling. In the half-light the guards assumed that the disguised king was the duke returning unexpectedly, and let them through. Uther made his way to Ygerna, convinced her that he was her husband, and had his way with her. Thus Arthur was conceived.

Meanwhile the real Gorlois, at Dimilioc, had been killed in a sortie. The identity of the man who had impregnated Ygerna would not be in any doubt. Uther's soldiers looted the camp, and it was not till morning that messengers went to Tintagel to report the outcome of the siege. Uther was still disguised. The messengers saw a person who was apparently Gorlois sitting in broad daylight with Ygerna beside him, and did not know what to make of it. Uther then left to return to his army, 'abandoning his disguise as Gorlois and becoming Uther Pendragon once more'. He was sorry that Gorlois was dead, but glad that Ygerna was free to marry and legitimate their offspring. From that day on, they lived together as equals: a remarkable acceptance on her part, considering that Uther had pursued her, deceived her and caused the death of her husband, together with an indefinite number of rank-and-file Cornishmen, all because of his irresponsible lust.

What was Geoffrey trying to do in this story, which gives Arthur such a discreditable beginning? If he made it all up, why did he make it up like that? Has any other author prepared the advent of a glorious hero, and then launched him with such a mixture of the disreputable and the absurd? And where does this leave Merlin, who masterminded the operation?

Consider the logic of composition, step by step, and the results. The plot requires that Uther, surrounded by his court, should single out an older man's wife and be instantly obsessed with her, neglecting his duties towards everybody else as king and host. He and Ygerna have to be brought together so that they can engender Arthur. But does she respond to his advances or not? If she does, she is unfaithful, and that won't do for Arthur's prospective mother. If she does not, his begetting of Arthur will be a kind of rape, and that won't do either. Very well, there must be an element of illusion or deception. Merlin must be enlisted again in a new capacity. A major feat of magical spellbinding would be out of keeping with the rest of the *History*. So he produces 'drugs', unprecedented and unspecified, that will change a man into a replica of another man. Uther can have access to Gorlois's wife because she will think he *is* Gorlois.

But what a mass of nonsense will have to be glossed over; and it will be nonsensical as nothing else in the *History* is. A change of appearance won't change everything. Uther can enter the castle, but he will have to find his way to the bedroom, and he can't ask a servant who thinks he is the lord of the castle and familiar with it. In the bedroom he will blunder against the furniture and not know where things are kept. Even in the dark his deception of Ygerna is incredible: his voice, his vocabulary, his mannerisms, all will expose him as a cosmetic impostor; she will ask him questions he can't answer; and − worst of all − he will have to imitate the sexual behaviour of a much older man whom he doesn't know very well, and who would not be in such a frenzy as is Uther himself.

Next morning, in daylight, the messengers must report the death of Gorlois. They know he is dead and have probably seen the body. They face the ostensible duke sitting with the duchess beside him, seemingly acquiescent, and . . . nothing happens. Nothing can happen. The logic of the plot has produced an impasse with no way out. Uther has to become himself again, so he 'abandons his disguise'. If drugs were needed to change him, surely drugs would be needed to change him back. Merlin, however, is no longer there. The reversal is effected somehow. As Ygerna's real husband is dead, she can become Uther's queen – his already pregnant queen – and await the birth of their magnificent son.

Geoffrey never perpetrates anything so preposterous in any other part of the *History*. Yet the origin of Arthur ought to be a supreme moment. One way to interpret this episode might be to suppose that he is retelling, and misguidedly trying to rationalise, an older myth now lost – a myth closer to some of the ancient Welsh stories in the *Mabinogion* which belong to a different world. Perhaps Merlin's prophetic spirit that takes possession of him is only one aspect of a greater entity, a tutelary god of Britain, who determines to create a hero for the island and manipulates the humans involved to bring it about. He gives Uther a passion for Gorlois's wife, which will reverse the effects of Vortigern's passion for the daughter of Hengist. He surrounds Tintagel with a web of illusion that negates ordinary perceptions and motivations. Perhaps Merlin, with his own strange birth, his unexplained comings and goings, and his lack of human relationships is an agent through whom the god works.

This of course is pure speculation. There is no evidence for such a myth, unless we count a vague medieval fancy that Tintagel Castle was enchanted, and became invisible every so often. However, there actually is evidence for belief in the god, or tutelary power, or whatever term seems apt. Tracing that belief may shed light on Merlin.

And one feature of the story does suggest that he has been used, and not only as a prophet, by an entity greater than himself: used as the contriver of Arthur's conception and immediately dismissed. At Dinas Emrys he lingers after the meeting with Vortigern. At Tintagel he does not linger; he disappears. Here tradition recognises him only as a phantom. At the base of the castle headland is a natural tunnel, starting from the cove and running through to an opening at the other end. This is Merlin's Cave. But he is not said to have lived in it, and he never could have, because it fills with water at high tide. His ghost haunts it, and that is all.

Merlin's exit from the *History* is one of the most surprising things in it. Later literature has accustomed us to the idea of his becoming Arthur's chief counsellor as the king grows up, and for years afterwards. The *History* has no hint of this. Merlin enters the castle with Uther to make sure that the amatory encounter happens, and once it has, he vanishes without a goodbye – and without even staying to help Uther undo his disguise. We are never told where he goes or what he does. We would expect him to reappear at intervals, keeping an eye on Arthur and perhaps prophesying for him. But he never does appear.* At Tintagel he has completed the assignment begun at Dinas Emrys. In this phase of his life, at least, it is certainly *as if* some higher power has employed him, taken control at crucial moments, and finally let him go.

* A brief reference to their meeting, further on in the *History*, is a mistake or an interpolation.

How far this view of him can be given substance remains to be seen. As a matter of fact, the attentive student of English literature can eventually find out where Merlin is during Uther's reign, and what he is doing. The answers, however, are in the work of an Elizabethan poet, Edmund Spenser.

4

KING ARTHUR

With the advent of Arthur, however awkwardly contrived, Geoffrey's *History* reached a point he had been building up to through many pages. At each step, Merlin had been the key figure, and without him there would have been no build-up at all. He had foreshadowed Arthur as the Boar of Cornwall, the leader who would give the red dragon a respite. He had enabled Aurelius Ambrosius to found a national monument on Salisbury Plain. He had interpreted the star portending the majesty of Uther's son. He had supplied Uther with the disguise that made the begetting of Arthur possible.

Then, his story broke off. Geoffrey went on to describe Arthur's marvellous career, without the marvellous counsellor who had stood beside his father and uncle. In spite of the *History*'s popularity, proved by hundred of manuscripts, Arthur's reign as Geoffrey described it could not lead to the flowering of medieval romance. It would create a framework for many flights of imagination, for a whole literature of chivalry and love and religion and war and magic. But not immediately. The development would happen through others, after several decades. First would come a more down-to-earth, quasi-historical phase.

When Geoffrey portrayed King Arthur, he was not writing in a void. In Wales and in what is now northern England, in

Cornwall and Brittany, traditions of Arthur had been current for a long time. There were chronicles with allusions to battles he was said to have fought – tantalisingly brief allusions, that have been scrutinised (and over-scrutinised) by historical inquirers searching for a real person behind the legend. There were tales and poems and genealogies. There were references to Arthur's wife and to his followers. There were anecdotes about his quarrels with ecclesiastics. For his own purpose, Geoffrey took whatever he felt able to use, and his fertile imagination augmented and organised whatever he took.

His intentions are easier to grasp if we see what he did *not* take. In particular, he kept largely clear of the earlier Welsh tales in the *Mabinogion*. As we saw, in the Dinas Emrys episode he was prepared to tell a story involving mysterious birth, prophecy and, in moderation, dragons. But he was not prepared to adopt the *Mabinogion*'s yarn of Lludd and Llevelys, telling how the dragons were closed in their casket and conveyed to Snowdonia, even though, without it, Merlin's knowledge of their presence was unexplained. The story of Merlin could be told so as to look something like history, even if it wasn't. The prequel about the alcoholic dragon-trap was grotesque, comic, a fairy-tale; it wouldn't do.

The same guiding principle can be seen more conspicuously in Geoffrey's rejection of Welsh Arthurian fiction. He is simply not *Mabinogion*-minded. One surviving Welsh tale of Arthur dates from before him. This is *Culhwch and Olwen* ('Culhwch' is pronounced Kil-hooch, with the *ch* as in 'loch'), and it is worth pausing over. Its verve and savagery, its fierce humour, its richness and colour and occasional beauty, belong to a milieu that is definitely pre-Geoffrey, and incompatible with his attitude. You cannot see it as an episode in the *History*.

The youth Culhwch in this tale is under a spell and cannot marry unless he wins Olwen, the daughter of Ysbaddaden, the Chief Giant. The seemingly fatal obstacle is that the giant is under a spell too, and is destined to die when his daughter weds. Several suitors have gone to ask for her hand and never returned. Culhwch decides to seek help from Arthur, who is his cousin, and 'chief lord of the island'. He sets off on a steed with a glossy grey head, four years old (translation by Jeffrey Gantz). . . .

> The lad sat on a precious gold saddle, holding a battle axe half a yard across from ridge to edge, an axe which would draw blood from the wind. . . . He had also a sword with a gold hilt and blade, a gold-chased buckler the colour of lightning, with an ivory boss, and two brindled white breasted greyhounds wearing red-gold collars from shoulder to ear. The greyhound on the right side would run to the left and the one on the left side would run to the right, and so they sported about him like two terns. . . . So smooth was his steed's gait that not a hair on his head stirred as he journeyed to Arthur's court.

The gatekeeper refuses to let him in, since everybody is at dinner, and offers inducements to go away and come back tomorrow, but Culhwch threatens to shout so loudly that pregnant women in the court will miscarry. When the gatekeeper goes off and reports, Arthur says Culhwch shouldn't be left outside in the wind and rain, and should be admitted and fed. So Culhwch rides his horse into the hall and asks for assistance in his bride-seeking. He calls upon Arthur's warriors for aid. The list is enormous. It runs to more than two hundred names, and includes a few genuine historical figures, some legendary ones, and a medley of fantastic and comic characters, including a man who can hold his breath under water for nine days, and another who can hear ants in the ground 50 miles away. A few have names that appear later in romances – Kay and Bedevere, for instance – but some that might be expected to appear do not. There is no Lancelot and there is no Tristan, though the ladies of the court include an Isolde.

Several of this early Arthurian host agree to go with Culhwch. They see the giant's fortress, and a shepherd and his wife give them discouraging accounts of previous ventures that ended badly. But Olwen, it transpires, comes out every Saturday to wash her hair, and they can try talking to her. She emerges in a blaze of colour, wearing a flame-coloured robe with a golden torque around her neck. Culhwch, she says, is welcome to try his luck, but her father will make demands which he must agree to, however far-fetched they seem.

They enter Ysbaddaden's hall. He tells them to come back later, then suddenly throws a poisoned spear at them. One of them catches it and throws it back, hitting the giant on the knee. 'Your cursed barbarian of a son-in-law!' he exclaims. 'Now it will be harder to walk uphill.' Two similar exchanges follow; each of them ought to be fatal to the giant, but he only complains of discomfort.

He consents to the marriage in principle, but tries to postpone it by making absurd conditions. Culhwch and his companions must carry out thirty-nine impossible tasks, such as ploughing and sowing a field, harvesting the crop, and making provisions for the wedding feast, all in one day. After many adventures, bringing in magic, talking animals and much else, and with Arthur himself participating, some at least of the giant's conditions are fulfilled – enough to count, apparently –

and an enemy cuts off Ysbaddaden's head and sets it on a stake. Olwen is not expected to go into mourning for her father, even with his severed head on display. Matrimony proceeds.

Geoffrey excluded all such exuberance from his book, in the interests of quasi-history. He wanted to give King Arthur something like a biography, in a literary setting that was something like a factual record; and despite all his forays into improbability, he managed to establish his version of Arthur in European minds. He attracted other writers. *The History of the Kings of Britain* was translated into Welsh, several times. These Welsh chronicles were called *Bruts*, after the name, Brutus, that stood at the beginning. More important for literature was a French *Roman de Brut* by the poet Wace, a native of Jersey who enjoyed the patronage of Henry II and Queen Eleanor. His verse paraphrase of the *History* appeared in 1155 and opened up the Arthurian field for many French-speaking readers. Wace was not credulous, nor inclined to encourage credulity. He was well aware – perhaps more so than Geoffrey – of the difficulty caused by recent Arthurian story-telling for anyone who cared about the facts: 'The tales of Arthur are not all lies nor all true. So much have the story-tellers told and so much have the makers of fables fabled to embellish their stories that they have made everything seem a fable.'

Wace did some investigating himself. He visited England, and gathered folklore in Brittany, including fairy lore in the forest of Broceliande, though he never actually saw any fairies, and was disappointed. In the *Roman de Brut* he shows some consideration for his readers, leaving out Merlin's prophecies and several passages of purely religious interest. He corrects Geoffrey on points of detail. He expands, sometimes lavishly and with fine poetic effect, drawing on other authors besides Geoffrey, and on oral tradition. He enhances many passages with dialogue and description. Pictorially, he can be vivid, as in an account of a fleet putting to sea, which reminds the reader that he was brought up in one of the Channel Islands, with a harbour.

Another follower of Geoffrey, and of Wace also, was the English poet Layamon, whose *Brut* – written considerably later – was even fuller than Wace's and in some ways more imaginative.

Here is a summary of the Arthur-without-Merlin history that Geoffrey, Wace and others established around the middle of the twelfth century. It may serve to show that while Merlin could be eliminated for a time, the full flow of romance, a few decades later, was almost bound to draw him back.

While Arthur was still a child, his father Uther contracted a lingering illness. He lived on for several years, but had to appoint Loth, the ruler of Lothian, as acting ruler from time to time. The Saxon chiefs Octa and Eosa, whom he held in prison, managed to escape and recruit a fresh army in Germany. Loth fought them indecisively; Uther, carried on a litter, went to attack the enemy at St Albans, and won a partial success. The Saxons, however, poisoned him (as they had poisoned his brother – Geoffrey's inventiveness could falter). Uther was buried inside the Giants' Ring.

On the advice of Dubricius, the Archbishop of Caerleon, Britain's leaders assembled at Silchester and crowned Uther's strangely begotten son, he being aged 15, but already mature. Silchester was a Roman town – we are still not far from the imperial order – and Arthur imitated new emperors in the past by distributing largesse to the troops. This action cemented their loyalty, but emptied the royal coffers. To replenish them, he set off for York to plunder the Saxons there. This was the less-than-glorious motive of Arthur's first campaign.

The Saxons had a new chief, Colgrin, who opposed him with Scottish and Pictish allies. Arthur besieged him in York. Colgrin's brother Baldulf got into the town by cutting off his hair and beard and pretending to be a non-combatant minstrel. Heartened by their reunion, the brothers forced Arthur to raise the siege.

Arthur withdrew to London and sent abroad for help. His cousin Hoel came over from Brittany, and the reinforced Britons moved to Lincoln, where they routed the Saxons and pursued them to the Celidon Wood in southern Scotland. Here Arthur first showed his military skill. He put his men to work felling trees and building barriers that blocked the opponents' access to their food supplies. They offered to hand over their treasure if Arthur would allow them to go back to their ships and return to Germany. He agreed, but they reneged on the deal and sailed round south-west Britain, landing, like others in the *History*, at Totnes, and marching rapidly to seize Bath.

Furious at their treachery, Arthur headed for the city. Archbishop Dubricius made a rousing speech to the soldiers, appealing, for the first time, to religion and what might now be called patriotism; Arthur's rule was creating a new spirit in his people. He put on a leather jerkin and a gold helmet, with a crest in the shape of a dragon. He carried a round shield with a picture of the Virgin Mary, and a long spear. But his principal weapon was a wonderful sword, Caliburn (not quite Excalibur yet), forged in the mysterious Isle of Avalon.

The Saxons were drawn up in wedge-shaped formations on a hill near the Roman city. Arthur's warriors succeeded in climbing the hill, but resistance was stubborn. Arthur drew Caliburn, called upon the name of the Blessed Virgin, and led a charge in person. Some 470 of the enemy were killed, and the Saxons were crushed at last. They dispersed in different directions. A general peace was in sight.

In the north the Picts and Scots had been aiding Arthur's enemies. As the triumphant Britons approached, their forces took refuge on the sixty islands in Loch Lomond, which, according to Geoffrey and Wace, were home to sixty eagles, one on each, who gathered annually to utter portentous shrieks. The authors add that the loch had sixty streams flowing into it, but only one flowing out to the sea. Arthur assembled a fleet of boats, cut off supplies to the islands, and forced the Picts and Scots to capitulate, meanwhile repulsing an Irish force that had come over to assist them. He treated these northern enemies with unprecedented severity, and accepted only an abject surrender.

While Cador, the Duke of Cornwall, chased the enemy remnants, Arthur and Hoel went on a sight-seeing tour around Loch Lomond. Hoel was surprised to find that everything was in sixties. Arthur told him of a perfectly square pool with four different kinds of fish in it, one species at each corner, and another pool near the Severn where the water almost vanished when the tide went down, and then shot up in a fountain when it rose again. His overseas cousin was suitably impressed.

Arthur proceeded to measures of restoration. He helped refugees to get their homes back, and rebuilt churches destroyed by the heathen. When the kingdom had settled down, he married Guinevere, Cador's beautiful daughter. His warfare was not quite done. He formed a fleet and conquered Ireland (foreshadowing, though he could not know it, centuries of trouble) and sailed on to conquer Iceland (which would not then have been difficult, since it was uninhabited).

Twelve years of peace and prosperity ensued. In this connection Wace makes an important point. Knowing of the many tales about Arthur and his followers, he realised that Geoffrey did not seem to have left much time for them to happen. He picked out the twelve-year Arthurian Peace as the one gap that would accommodate them. 'During the long peace of which I speak – I know not whether you have heard of it – the wonders were demonstrated and the adventures were found which are so often related of Arthur that they have been turned into a fable.' The need for an Arthurian Peace for adventures to happen in would be carried over from Wace into medieval romance. As the adventures multiplied, so the Peace became longer, till some of the characters were given improbably long lives.

Another product of the Arthurian Peace was the institution of the Round Table, which Geoffrey does not mention, but Wace does. Wace seems to think that it may have been a Breton invention: it could have originated in a Celtic custom, when warriors stood in a circle with their chief. The purpose of Arthur's Round Table was practical. When his nobles sat down at it, they would all be equal, none above another. The mystical meanings that became attached to it later came in with the reappearance of Merlin.

With or without the specific item of furniture, Arthur inaugurated an order of knighthood that was a first step towards the ceremonial Round Table of later times. He was founding a sort of aristocratic Foreign Legion.

Arthur then began to increase his personal entourage by inviting very distinguished men from far distant kingdoms to join it. In this way he developed such a code of courtliness in his household that he inspired peoples living far away to imitate him. . . . At last the famè of Arthur's generosity and bravery spread to the very ends of the earth; and the kings of countries far across the sea trembled at the thought that they might be attacked and invaded by him, and so lose control of the lands under their dominion.

Aware of the awe he was inspiring, Arthur took what amounted to a hint, and annexed Norway and Denmark. Those countries had never been Roman. However, the Roman Empire still existed and it set him wondering. Under a fourth-century constitutional arrangement, it was divided into eastern and western portions. At that time the eastern emperor at Constantinople was Leo. There was a vacancy in the west, where Gaul was governed in Leo's name by a deputy with the curious name Frollo. Arthur set out to conquer Gaul. Britain, in Roman eyes, was still nominally a tribute-paying province, but he had stopped paying tribute and considered himself independent. He took an army across the Channel, having subsidised Gallic leaders so that most of them did not join Frollo to oppose him. The war was settled in epic style by a single combat: Arthur brought Caliburn down on Frollo's head, and split it. Most of Gaul submitted, but it was a large country and the reorganisation under British rule was a long-term project requiring, in the end, nine years. His principal knights, Kay and Bedevere, became regional viceroys.

At Whitsun Arthur held a plenary court with a ceremonial crown-wearing, at the Roman city of Caerleon in Wales. All the nobility and higher clergy attended. Geoffrey's account, long and picturesque, is notable for something it does *not* say. His

Arthurian Britain is still geographically Roman Britain. Camelot, Arthur's non-Roman headquarters in romance, is not yet in sight. Caerleon, a place surely familiar to anyone from Geoffrey's Monmouth, was a major legionary base with a fine amphitheatre and many other buildings.

Geoffrey and Wace give long lists of eminent people who attended the ceremony. Several are regional kings – of Scotland, North and South Wales, Cornwall – giving the impression that Arthur is pictured as a High King on the Irish model, with lesser kings under him. Other guests are rulers from overseas. Several pages of elaborate description evoke the scene; this is something that Geoffrey can be good at. In a famous paragraph anticipating the tales of chivalry, he says:

> Britain had reached such a standard of sophistication that it excelled all other kingdoms in its general affluence, the richness of its decorations, and the courteous behaviour of its inhabitants. Every knight in the country who was in any way famed for his bravery wore livery and arms showing his own distinctive colour; and women of fashion often displayed the same colours. They scorned to give their love to any man who had not proved himself three times in battle. In this way the womenfolk became chaste and more virtuous and for their love the knights were ever more daring.

Contests in archery, lance-tossing and weight-hurling were interrupted by the arrival of twelve men carrying olive branches. They were envoys from Lucius Hiberius, who was now emperor in the west, though he styled himself Procurator of the Republic. He protested at Arthur's aggressions and withholding of tribute, and demanded his submission to Rome with a threat of war. Arthur summoned a meeting of his chief subordinates, Cador, Hoel, King Auguselus of Scotland, and others. He justified his rejection of the Roman demand by citing the precedent planted further back in the *History*: two British rulers, Belinus and Brennius, had captured Rome and extorted tribute themselves; Arthur would have every right to do likewise. Hoel produced a prophecy that another Briton would be master of Rome.

All agreed that the best mode of defence was attack. From his various territories, the king collected an army of more than a hundred thousand. Lucius Hiberius assembled a mixed imperial force drawn from several provinces. Arthur appointed Queen Guinevere and his nephew Modred as regents during his absence abroad, and crossed the Channel again.

Modern Arthurian writers tend to push this Roman embroilment into the background. It obviously never happened; it isn't interesting; none of the famous episodes takes place in a continental setting. Yet Geoffrey, giving the Arthurian legend this primary form, certainly *did* think the Gallic part important. Assessed by the amount of space he gave it, his Arthur is at least as much a Gallic conqueror as anything else. Wace does not think otherwise.

On the way to confront Lucius's army, Arthur learned that Hoel's niece Helena had been kidnapped by a giant from Spain who had made his home on Mont-Saint-Michel in Normandy — a counterpart of the giant Cormoran on St Michael's Mount in Cornwall. Geoffrey devotes several pages to a fight with the giant, an attempt, possibly, to bring some colourful fantasy into a story that was too purely historical, or at least quasi-historical. But the giant is rather tedious, and the narrative only regains momentum when the armies clash. Another of the better-known characters, Arthur's nephew Gawain, becomes prominent here.

King Arthur defeated and killed Lucius, marched into Burgundy, and planned an attack on the eastern emperor Leo himself. Then news from home checked him. This (a fact hardly ever pointed out) is one place in the *History*, the only place, where Geoffrey mentions something specific as coming from his 'ancient book'. It is the only clue to what the book actually said, if it existed and he didn't simply invent it. What had happened – and there is an echo here of authentic Welsh tradition – was that Arthur's deputy in Britain, Modred, had turned traitor and persuaded the queen to live in adultery with him.

Arthur cancelled his plans and rushed back to Britain, where Modred had not only declared himself king but had also enlisted Saxons in support of his revolt. Arthur landed and pushed Modred's army back to Winchester. Guinevere succumbed to guilt and despair, and entered a convent. The conflict ended in a battle which the Welsh call Camlan; Geoffrey locates it by the River Camel in Cornwall. Modred was killed and the revolt collapsed.

So ends the story of Arthur's reign. But even Geoffrey, with all his air of historicity, could not allow Arthur to perish. He had to leave room for the popular belief among the Welsh, Cornish and Bretons (especially the Bretons) that Arthur never died and might return. He had accepted from the beginning that Arthur's departure would be mysterious; that was in Merlin's prophecies. Now he closed the reign after the final battle with a profound ambiguity: 'Arthur himself, our renowned king, was mortally wounded and was carried off to the Isle of Avalon, so that his wounds might be attended to.' Geoffrey had named Avalon once, as the place where Arthur's sword was forged, without any clue to its location. No prospective return is mentioned.

Wace confirms, and ventures a little further:

He is yet in Avalon, awaited of the Britons; for as they say and deem he will return from whence he went and live again. Master Wace, the writer of this book, cannot add more to this matter of his end than was spoken by Merlin the Prophet. Merlin said of Arthur – if I read it right – that his end should be hidden in doubtfulness. . . . Men have ever doubted, and – as I am persuaded – will always doubt whether he liveth or is dead.

Shortly before Wace wrote, however, and without his knowledge, Geoffrey himself had sprung a surprise.

Note

When is all this supposed to have happened?

The problem of the 'historical Arthur' is not involved here. Various indications spread out his hypothetical career over an impossible period, a hundred years or more, and a would-be historian has to decide whereabouts in the range to put him, if he should be put anywhere. My personal belief is that an 'original Arthur' can be identified as the starting-point of the legend. That, however, is not the present question. The present question concerns Geoffrey of Monmouth's intentions, which need to be defined for the evaluation of issues that he raises.

Data such as his anachronisms with chivalry, courtly conduct and other matters are of no value as evidence. Medieval writers and artists, portraying a time in the distant past, did not aim at authenticity like a modern historical novelist. They updated customs, clothing and many other aspects to make their characters look like contemporaries. Only the overall setting is significant here.

For Vortigern, Geoffrey gives a chronological 'fix' — that is, a statement calibrating the *History* with known fact:

> It was at this time that St Germanus, the Bishop of Auxerre, came, and Lupus, Bishop of Troyes, to preach the word of God to the Britons.

Germanus's British mission, aimed at eliminating the Pelagian heresy, was in 429. Therefore Vortigern was in power then, and his royal victim King Constantine is supposed to have been murdered before that. Constantine's son Aurelius becomes king a little after Vortigern's short reign, and does not last long himself, dying, by inference, in the early 430s. His brother Uther succeeds him and begets Arthur soon afterwards. Arthur cannot be born much after 440 at the latest.

Arthur's whole reign occurs while the Roman Empire is still in existence, with a western and an eastern part. There is still an emperor of sorts in Rome (Lucius, despite his odd title, is occasionally called so). After 476 there was no emperor in Rome, so Arthur is earlier. Geoffrey names the eastern emperor during his reign as Leo, three times. He can only be Leo I, who reigned from 457 to 474.

A study of medieval texts by Professor Barbara Moorman has shown that there was a chronicle tradition independent of Geoffrey, giving Arthur a reign extending from about 454 to 470. This agrees with Geoffrey's own indications. However, he causes confusion by naming people outside the range, and the chronological question has been bedevilled by a passage in the extant text of the *History* putting the departure of Arthur in 542. This is completely incompatible with everything else, and its air of exactitude is misleading. It has to be a mistake, and in fact it has been shown that the 'wild' date 542 could have been produced by recognised processes of error, the true date being, consistently, 470.* Wace shows the insubstantiality of 542 by putting the departure of Arthur in 642.

* See Ashe, *The Discovery of King Arthur* (Stroud: Sutton Publishing, 2003), pp. 103–4, 111–16, 213–14.

5

ḦOW MANY MERLINS?

G eoffrey of Monmouth drops Merlin as soon as Arthur is
safely conceived. He drops him unceremoniously, leaving
him at Tintagel without even extricating him from the
castle. But Merlin would not stay dropped. Presently, the
glaring presence of a post-Merlin void, together with new
information, pushed Geoffrey toward a sequel.

During the fifth and sixth centuries Britain was fragmented.
In the western part of the island, there were successor kingdoms
of unsubdued Britons: Gwynedd, Powys, Dumnonia. In the
eastern part there were kingdoms of Anglo-Saxons, incipient
English: Kent, Essex, East Anglia. A nascent Wessex, the realm
of the West Saxons, was starting on the way to its destiny as the
nucleus of the United Kingdom. The English were advancing,
but not spectacularly. The north was more chaotic and more
confusing. There were kingdoms of Britons in Cumbria and
Strathclyde; there was a kingdom of Scots in Argyll; there were
Picts everywhere.

Christianity had spread beyond the converted ex-Roman
territories and was gradually gaining ground in the north,
owing especially to one man, St Kentigern, nicknamed Mungo.
A Briton by birth, his life was tumultuous; he moved from place
to place, harassed by enemies; for a time he was a refugee in
Wales. At length he established himself in Glasgow, then a very

small settlement indeed. When it grew greater, he was adopted as the city's patron. Further travels took him into the Forest of Celidon between Clyde and the present border.

Early accounts of Kentigern describe a strange meeting. One day when he was praying alone, in a solitary place in the woods, a crazy half-naked man came running towards him. This man was named Lailoken. Kentigern asked him who he was and why he was wandering like this, living among the beasts of the wilderness. Lailoken replied that he was a Christian, but a bad one. He was undergoing lifelong penance for his guilt in stirring up a battle that took many lives. At that time he had seen a vision in the sky of armed men threatening him, and heard a heavenly voice condemning him to the miserable existence that Kentigern witnessed. He had endured many years of it, and was old.

They parted. Later, the crazy man would sit on a hillock overlooking Glasgow, shouting and lamenting, to the distraction of Kentigern and his community. Lailoken was blessed or cursed with second sight, and uttered prophecies which no one took seriously. A day came when he foresaw his own death and wished to receive the sacrament. Kentigern, who did not then recollect who he was, sent a priest to ask about his anticipations of death, and see whether they made sense. He was known to have spoken in the same style before, incoherently and inconsistently. Sometimes he expected to die by being impaled, sometimes by drowning. But Kentigern gave him the benefit of the doubt and let him receive the sacrament. He was partly restored to sanity, and Kentigern finally realised who he was. Though reconciled with the Church, he still prophesied, predicting, among other things, the imminent death of some of the nobles of the kingdom. He returned to the forest. Through some odd coincidences, his self-contradictory forebodings were all fulfilled.

Another document tells how a local king kidnapped Lailoken, had him tied up, and tried to extort prophecies from him. Lailoken gave riddling answers, hinting at the infidelity of the king's wife. She tried to reassure her husband, but he believed the prophet, and she decided to have Lailoken killed. Some shepherds carried out her wish. And this unhinged northerner was called something else besides Lailoken. He was called Merlin.

He came to be talked about and remembered in Wales by the pre-Geoffrey form of the name, Myrddin, and was viewed respectfully. He may be the Myrddin who is cited in the 'Omen of Britain' poem which Geoffrey knew, predicting British recovery, though that is not certain. He was counted among the bards. No authentic poem by him survives, but Welshmen circulated verses he was supposed to have uttered – dramatic monologues, so to speak. They embedded scraps of nostalgic lamentation in semi-political outpourings. One such pseud-onymous poem is 'The Apple Tree':

> Sweet apple tree, that grows by a river bank . . .
> While I was calm in mind I used to sit at its base
> With a fair-playful maiden, a slender and queenly one. . . .
> In constraint of outlawry
> I have been wandering with wildness and wild ones.
> After irreproachable goods and pleasing minstrels,
> Now there visit only want with wildness and wild ones.

In another poem he is made to address a pig, his sole companion. He recalls his friendship with the King of Strathclyde:

Little knows Rhydderch Hael tonight at his feast
What I endured last night of sleeplessness:
Snow up to my knees; overgrowth like a pack of hounds;
Icicles in my beard.

Geoffrey had read the 'Omen of Britain' in which he noticed
'Myrddin' without any idea who Myrddin was. But in 1152 he
was appointed Bishop of St Asaph in Wales, and its monks had
a copy of a life of St Kentigern. Probably from this Geoffrey
learned about Lailoken, the Myrddin in the north. When
composing 'Merlin's Prophecies' long before, he had simply
taken Myrddin from the 'Omen of Britain' as a name having
something to do with prophecy, and attached it, respelt, to the
person at Dinas Emrys without knowing or caring where it
came from. But now he discovered Lailoken, a real prophet in a
particular place far from Dinas Emrys. Had he made a wrong
guess? Not necessarily. The two might be the same. He decided
to put together a single story, with the prophet, long after the
History events, taking the stage again in a northern sequel based
on northern material.

His new story was called *Vita Merlini*, the Life of Merlin, and
it was written in Latin hexameter verse, quite good by medieval
standards. To some extent it was a literary *jeu d'esprit*, not aimed
at a large readership like the *History* – and it never acquired one.
There is only a single extant manuscript.

A present-day reader will see two manifest objections to this
project, one illusory, the other serious. Present-day readers (it is
worth reiterating) are conditioned by Tennyson, Disney and
others to picture Merlin as a bearded ancient with a conical hat
and a long, elegant robe: hardly a person to be portrayed
wandering about insane and dishevelled in a Scottish wilderness.

But (it is also worth reiterating) Merlin in Geoffrey's *History* is not like that. Having appeared first as a boy, he is still youthful when he bows out after the Tintagel affair. He has two prophetic seizures, and a more fundamental one would be consistent and credible.

The other difficulty about this sequel is that the chronology is wrong. The main characters, including the northern Myrddin himself, seem to have flourished in the late sixth century. Geoffrey is perfectly capable of fudging dates. In this case, by concentrating on the northern traditions and soft-pedalling his own *History*, he forestalls any attempt to compare his books too closely. He tries to hold everything together with a speech by the aged Merlin reminiscing about the long-ago meeting with Vortigern, and recalling events in the *History* right through to the reign of Arthur, his campaigns and betrayal, and his mysterious passing. Merlin reviews all these happenings, though he barely mentions his own part in them. However, the passage is not a real attempt to harmonise. That would simply be impossible, the gap is too wide to bridge. He has to ignore the real dating of Vortigern and the implied dating of Arthur, and mix everything together in a sort of post-Arthurian limbo.

He begins the *Vita Merlini* by telling the reader that after an unspecified lapse of time Merlin became famous not only as a prophet but as the ruler of South Wales, in the break-up of Arthur's kingdom. He summarises traditions relating how the northern king Peredur made war on a kinsman named Gwenddolau. Merlin, he says, left South Wales to accompany Peredur's army, and another king, Rhydderch (the one who is mentioned in the 'pig' poem), was also drawn in. Hence the battle mentioned in the Life of St Kentigern which drove Merlin mad, the battle of Arfderydd or Arthuret. This is a real place, which can be located on the north side of Longtown parish, near Gwenddolau's stronghold Caer Gwenddolau – a name later corrupted into 'Carwhinelow' and eventually 'Carwinley'. Carwinley today is a quiet spot among woods and low hills, with traces of early fortifications nearer to Liddell Water.

Since Peredur and Gwenddolau were kinsmen, the battle had the special tragedy of a civil war. It was remembered in later years, with bitter humour, as a 'frivolous' or 'futile' battle fought over a lark's nest. The dispute in fact was about Caerlaverock, the Fort of the Lark, on the north side of the Solway Firth. The carnage was frightful, and several leaders were killed. Geoffrey describes in painful detail how Merlin's mind gave way and he rushed off into the Forest of Celidon. However, he eventually became friendly with King Rhydderch and was received at his court, though he was not enthusiastic about staying there. He still had glimpses of the future.

Rhydderch's queen Ganieda was Merlin's sister. His wanderings had separated them for a long time, and he insinuated that she was unfaithful to her husband. She did not contemplate violence as in the older version, but she wanted to discredit him in Rhydderch's eyes, so she set up a test. She brought a boy to her brother and asked how he would die. Merlin said he would fall from a high rock. She took the boy away, had his hair cut, dressed him differently and brought him back; Merlin said he would perish violently in a tree. She brought him again disguised as a woman; Merlin said he would die in a river. Since it was actually the same boy each time, Ganieda convinced Rhydderch that her brother was wrong and he had nothing to worry about. However, when the boy grew up and went out hunting, his horse slipped on a rock. He fell down a precipice into a river, caught his foot in a tree, and was drowned.

Merlin continued to spend much time in the woods, under the compulsion of his controlling spirit. In the grip of this being – now conceived as much more than a spirit of prophecy alone – he had preternatural knowledge. He was to speak of it in unhappy retrospect: 'I knew the secrets of things and the flight of birds and the wandering motion of the stars and the gliding of the fishes.' His quasi-omniscience was not a gift but a torment: 'All this vexed me and denied a natural rest to my human mind.' When the power possessed him, he had wild ideas. Ganieda persuaded him to come indoors during the winter, and he agreed to have a house built for him. But he asked her for a separate observatory with seventy doors and seventy windows, and resident scribes to record his observations.

❖

Merlin sent for Taliesin, the chief of the bards, wanting to consult him about the weather, a subject on which Taliesin was an expert – as he was on many other subjects. Taliesin was a real person, probably born in Wales, but he wandered. Poems attributed to him include some that are authentically his, the oldest verses in any living language of Europe apart from Greek. Welsh tradition credits him as well as Merlin with prophetic powers.

A fantastic 'Story of Taliesin' makes his birth supernatural. His original name was Gwion; he was the beautiful but unwanted child of a witch, who tied him up in a leather bag and threw him into the sea. He was saved by Elphin, a nephew of Maelgwn, King of Gwynedd in North Wales. Elphin called the foundling Taliesin, meaning 'radiant brow', and fostered him.

While Taliesin was still a boy, Maelgwn imprisoned Elphin at Deganwy near Llandudno. Taliesin came to rescue him, and achieved this by baffling the court poets. He cast a spell so that they could only say *blerwm blerwm*, and, assured of an uninterrupted hearing, recited a complicated and seemingly insoluble riddle. As presented, it looks like a series of statements by Taliesin about himself — about previous incarnations, perhaps. But each statement may refer to a different person, and if they were all identified, the result might be a cipher message or acrostic. These lines are a fair sample:

> My original country is the region of the summer stars . . .
> I was with my Lord in the highest sphere,
> On the fall of Lucifer into the depth of hell;
> I have borne a banner before Alexander;
> I know the names of the stars from north to south;
> I have been on the Galaxy at the throne of the Distributor;
> I was in Canaan when Absalom was slain;
> I conveyed Awen to the level of the vale of Hebron . . .
> I was instructor to Eli and Enoch . . .
> I have been three periods in the prison of Arianrhod;
> I have been the chief director of the work of the tower of
>   Nimrod . . .
> I have been in Asia with Noah in the Ark,
> I have witnessed the destruction of Sodom and Gomorrah.

And so on. Robert Graves claimed to have solved the riddle, and made his solution the cornerstone of his study of poetic myth, *The White Goddess*.

Guided by Minerva, a surprising divine associate, Taliesin deluges Merlin with pseudo-scientific lore about climates, the sea and the creatures living in it. Geoffrey seems to include this lecture for his own amusement, but towards the end Taliesin adds some geography, describing various islands: Britain itself, the Orkneys (thirty-three of them), Thule in arctic gloom, Ireland, and so on. He ends the list with a truly memorable one, the enchanted apple-island, Avalon, already mentioned in *The History of the Kings of Britain* as Arthur's last earthly destination:

> The island of apples which men call 'The Fortunate Isle' gets its name from the fact that it produces all things of itself. Of its own accord it produces grain and grapes, and apple trees grow in its woods from the close-clipped grass. . . . People live there a hundred years or more. There nine sisters rule by a pleasing set of laws those who come to them from our country. She who is first of these is more skilled in the healing art and excels her sisters in the beauty of her person. Morgen is her name. . . . She also knows an art by which to change her shape and to cleave the air on new wings like Daedalus; when she wishes she is at Brest, Chartres, or Pavia, and when she will she slips down from the air on your shores. And men say that she has taught mathematics to her sisters.

This is the literary debut of Morgen, who becomes Morgan le Fay in Arthurian romances. Her name means 'sea-born'. She is a humanised goddess, and her community resembles actual pagan sisterhoods, such as a group of nine wonder-working healers who lived on the Ile de Sein off the coast of Brittany.

Taliesin proceeds, making the story personal and detailed:

> Thither after the battle of Camlan we took the wounded Arthur, guided by Barinthus to whom the waters and the stars of heaven were well known. . . . Morgen received us with fitting honour, and in her chamber she placed the

king on a golden bed and with her own hand she uncovered his honourable wound and gazed at it for a long time. At length she said that his health could be restored to him if he stayed with her for a long time and made use of her healing art. Rejoicing, therefore, we entrusted the king to her and returning spread our sails to the favouring winds.

The pilot Barinthus is a figure from Irish legend, whose talk of the western ocean inspired the maritime exploits of St Brendan 'the Navigator'.

Merlin, having listened to Taliesin attentively, mourns that since the passing of Arthur the Britons have fought among themselves and the Saxons can be expected to renew their advance. Taliesin offers the remarkable suggestion that if Arthur has recovered, a deputation should visit Avalon, and invite him to come back to Britain and rule again. This is not the mystical hope of the return of Arthur that lingered into modern times; it is an immediate, practical proposal. Incidentally it assumes a more or less reunited Britain, which Arthur ruled and could rule again; if this anachronism were made to date the text, it would throw the story into chaos. Merlin, however, rejects the idea. The Saxons must prevail. There will be no British victory in the lifetime of anyone living.

While he is speaking, and reviewing past misfortunes, news is brought of a spring gushing out suddenly below a nearby hill. Merlin sees the clear water flowing, and, on impulse, drinks some of it and washes his face – whereupon the madness drops from him for ever. 'He regained his reason and knew himself, and all his madness departed and the sense which had long remained torpid in him revived, and he remained what he had once been – sane and intact with his reason restored.'

He cares no more about his prophetic gift, or the torturing knowledge that accompanied it. Now, he declares, he has come to himself. He is free and reinvigorated. He gives thanks to God and vows fidelity to him. Taliesin, clearly a compulsive lecturer, responds with another discourse, this time about the rivers and lakes in various countries and the different properties of the waters.

Reports are soon spreading of the new spring and Merlin's return to sanity. The nobles of the land urge him to take up his royal power again, but he replies that he is too old, he will be content with a quiet life in the forest. Maeldinus, a madman, also drinks the spring-water and becomes sane. He at once expresses a wish to stay with Merlin in retirement. Taliesin himself announces that he will turn away from the world and join them, and so does Ganieda. She utters a few prophecies herself, ending with a prayer to Christ to give peace to the people. Her brother acknowledges that the prophetic spirit, which has closed his own mouth, may still speak occasionally through hers without harm. The quartet – Merlin, his sister, Taliesin the bard and Maeldinus – live together in harmony.

Geoffrey takes the story no further. None of his chief characters dies. However, the Merlin of the northern tradition, Myrddin or Lailoken, does have a grave. This is not an instance of what some Americans call 'fakelore': the place is already indicated in the Life of St Kentigern. It is at Drumelzier in Tweeddale, between the road and the river. Here the valley broadens out, and the adjoining hills draw away from the Tweed. Merlin's grave is beside a burn, the Pausayl or Powsail (the name means 'Willow'), which runs rapidly downhill under trees and around the base of a bluff. After this, it flows more gently through level meadows to a confluence with the Tweed.

Merlin's grave is supposed to be near a tree at the foot of the bluff. However, an alternative site is in the corner of a field by the river, where there used to be a cairn. The Pausayl does not flow that way now, but is said to have changed course during a spate in 1603, when James VI of Scotland became also James I of England. According to a verse ascribed to the medieval seer Thomas the Rhymer,

> When Tweed and Pausayl meet at Merlin's grave,
> Scotland and England shall one monarch have.

The valley floor is so flat that a change of course would have been possible.

A legend that accounts for this grave is a variation on the 'triple death' theme which Geoffrey adapts in the *Vita Merlini*. The prophet incited some tribesmen to revolt, unsuccessfully and with serious loss of life, against the British rulers of Strathclyde. For his guilt, he was condemned to be a perpetual wanderer. He made predictions about his own death that sounded contradictory. He would fall from a cliff, he would be hanged, he would drown. All three forecasts were correct. When shepherds threatened him with violence, he threw himself from a cliff into the Tweed. His feet became tangled in salmon nets and he hung head down in the water till he drowned. His name survives locally in a place called Merlindale, over the bridge across the river.

Wiltshire too has a grave of Merlin, at Marlborough, and its distance from Drumelzier is significant. It is not a rival, because its supposed occupant is Merlin Ambrosius, the earlier Merlin of

Geoffrey's *History*. In the Middle Ages the place-name Marlborough was sometimes Latinised in the form 'Merlebergia'. The grave is a high artificial mound in the grounds of Marlborough College, called Merlin's Mount. In 1215 Alexander Neckham, the abbot of Cirencester, wrote: 'Merlin's tumulus gave you your name, Merlebergia.' The Mount is terraced, but its present shape is due at least partly to remodelling in the seventeenth century. A small Norman castle once stood on the top, but it may be prehistoric in its origins. Coins of William the Conqueror give the town's name as 'Maerlebi' and 'Maerliber', but Neckham's derivation is due to a misunderstanding, because the spelling of the prophet's name with an L – 'Merlin' instead of 'Myrddin' – is unknown before Geoffrey in the 1130s: that is, after the coins.

The distance and difference between the two graves underlines a distinction that became orthodox. Geoffrey's attempt to merge the northerner with the Snowdonian prophet could never have been convincing, and in practice it failed to convince. Giraldus Cambrensis asserted the common-sense view that there were two Merlins, both real – Merlin Ambrosius or Emrys, who confronted Vortigern, and Merlin Celidonius, otherwise Silvester, the dweller in Scottish forests. Welsh writers after Giraldus accept the distinction. The Merlin of literary romance and legend, who, notoriously, becomes a magician, is the first of the two.

And yet, despite acceptance that Myrddin Emrys and Myrddin Celidonius were historically distinct, a feeling persisted that they were linked by more than Geoffrey's imagination; that the shared spirit of prophecy was one aspect of a more fundamental bond. In a series of elegies under the title *Gododdin*, attributed to the poet Aneirin and assigned (at least in substance) to the year 600 or thereabouts, a verse refers to the *awen* of Myrddin. *Awen* meant bardic inspiration. The author of the *Armes Prydein*, the aforementioned 'Omen of Britain' composed about 930, cites Myrddin and *awen* as forecasting British revival, and they seem almost interchangeable.

Numerous Welsh traditions are preserved in 'triads', which summarise topics in sets of three. One triad names 'three skilful bards': the northerner Myrddin, Myrddin Emrys and Taliesin. A sixteenth-century Welshman, Elis Gruffudd, makes the amazing yet revealing claim that the three bards shared a single identity. They were the same being in three incarnations. In the fabulous *Story of Taliesin*, the young poet prefaces his famous riddle with a personal introduction:

My prophetic country is the region of the summer stars.
The Prophet Johannes called me Myrddin.
But now all kings know me as Taliesin.

As in the triad, Myrddin and Taliesin seem to be identified, whether or not through reincarnation.

Both the Myrddins, it should be stressed, have personal names of their own. One of them is Emrys or Ambrosius, the other is Lailoken, and they are far apart in space and time, with no visible connection. Yet 'Myrddin' is attached to both. Moreover, it has the air of a sobriquet that enhances its recipient. Lailoken-as-Myrddin in the literary tradition is a person of greater stature and dignity than Lailoken is himself. He is more than a pitiable lunatic. Poetic speech is put in his mouth, and he becomes a serious oracle. Myrddin Emrys, too, is vastly more than the local boy-seer Ambrosius.

If 'Myrddin' had this quality of connection, extension and expansion, what does it mean, where did it come from? Etymology confirms the impression. It is not, originally, a personal name at all. It apparently began as a British place-name, Moridunon (Latinised as Moridunum), meaning 'sea-fortress'. In Welsh this became 'Myr-ddin'. At some stage – no one knows when – the prefix 'Caer', meaning a fortress or stronghold, was prefixed to it, as at other places such as Caernarvon. But 'Caer' with 'Myrddin' was tautological – the 'fortress-sea-fortress' – and the 'Myrddin' part was interpreted as the name of a man, so the place became 'the fortress of Myrddin'. The name in English is 'Carmarthen'. So we know, finally, where we are.

It might be argued that Myrddin was a completely fictitious character, invented to account for the place-name in its final form, and identified, as a mistaken afterthought, with someone who happened to be born there. But this would not explain why 'Myrddin' came to be attached also to Lailoken, far away from South Wales. For some reason it had a connotation; it was associated with the 'spirit of prophecy' linking the two figures; and, applied to those two, it became a designation and even perhaps an honorific.

Merlin Ambrosius, as presented in *The History of the Kings of Britain*, is born in Carmarthen. (Geoffrey would like us to think that the place was named after him, but the truth is the other way round.) In this case the connection is immediate, and legend gives him local associations. A rhyme linked Carmarthen's fortunes with Merlin's Tree, the Priory Oak, that was once in the centre:

> When Myrddin's Tree shall tumble down,
> Then shall fall Carmarthen town.

The civic authorities braced the tree with iron supports, and later removed it to the local museum.

Some 2½ miles up the valley of the Tywi or Towy is Bryn Myrddin, Merlin's Hill, an abrupt rise on the north side of the main road. A wood near it is Merlin's Grove. On the other side of the road is Merlin's Stone, which once fell on a treasure-seeker and crushed him, fulfilling a prophecy that a raven would drink human blood off the stone; a team of five horses was needed to restore it to an upright position. There is also the legend of Merlin's Cave – another one. Tintagel's is better known. This one is said to be a natural chamber concealed in the lower part of the hill. Merlin was trapped in it by a woman he loved. She learned magic spells from him and used them to imprison him. The story is an offshoot of later romance, but it has a twist of its own: that he is still in the cave alive, and if you listen in the right place you can hear him groaning.

Carmarthen's local lore is unlikely to be ancient, let alone prehistoric, but Wales supplies something else that is: a link between the Myrddins immeasurably older than any historical factors in the fifth and sixth century.

Embedded in a Welsh manuscript, the *White Book of Rhydderch*, there is a summary of British prehistory which is certainly prior to Geoffrey, perhaps a long way prior, and which he either never knew or suppressed as incompatible with his giants and Trojans. It is headed 'These are the Names of the Island of Britain'. The opening paragraph runs as follows:

The first name that this Island bore, before it was taken or settled: Myrddin's Precinct. And after it was taken and settled, the Island of Honey. And after it was conquered by Prydein son of Aedd the Great it was called the Island of Prydein (Britain).

In the second sentence, 'Island of Honey', *Y Vel Ynys*, looks odd. According to Rachel Bromwich, the leading authority on early Welsh texts, the normal form would be *Ynys Vel*, and this may have been a corruption of *Ynys Veli*, meaning the Island of Beli – Beli being a mythical ancestor of dynasties. However that may be, the first sentence is the arresting one. The word translated 'precinct', *Clas*, has various meanings and might be translated 'enclosure'; a better attested Greek equivalent is *temenos*. This is a plain statement that the island was Myrddin's *before* it had any human population, and if so then Myrddin in this context has to be more than human – a god.

Dr Bromwich remarks that 'it is difficult to account for the association of the name of Myrddin with this tradition'. That is putting it mildly. No one could suppose that thousands of years ago the island of Britain, as yet uninhabited (presumably because Noah's descendants had not yet reached it), was called by a name derived from someone in the still-remote Christian era. The prophetic designation must have been related to something far earlier – to the cult or myth of a senior being who could properly be given the same designation. All of a sudden we may be face to face with the tutelary god of Britain suggested in Chapter 3, whose myths might underlie some of Geoffrey's more peculiar notions.

This being's real or principal name could not actually have been Myrddin, He-of-Moridunum, before Moridunum existed. But British bards or story-tellers could have applied it to him in retrospect, when he had a special association with the place. He could have had a major cultic centre or shrine in that area, with a numinosity extending over south-west Wales. Carmarthen is less than 20 miles from the bluestone quarry in the Prescelly Mountains. The bluestones were the first architectural components of Stonehenge, forming the primary circle long before the tall sarsens. They were apparently imported from south-west Wales as the basic constituents of the great social and ceremonial centre. Why from there, with such a colossal expenditure of effort? What was unique about them? Could it have been because south-west Wales was the main territory of Britain's tutelary god? And their journey over the sea from the west was correctly ascribed by Geoffrey to Merlin, otherwise Myrddin.

One aspect of this god would have been the spirit of prophecy, emanating perhaps from a centre in the Carmarthen area. Persons inspired by him, and delivering mantic utterances, became Myrddin's-men (or women – let us not forget Ganieda) – or simply Myrddins. The Greeks had a deity who inspired and possessed his devotees, if in a rather more abandoned way; this deity was named Dionysos or Bacchos, and a person whom he inspired or possessed could be called a Bacchos.

Geoffrey of Monmouth, after centuries of Christianity, no longer has the clue. He is aware of a plurality of Myrddins, or, to use his own spelling, Merlins, and tries to unite them by fancying that the builder of Stonehenge, the fifth-century seer and the sixth-century wanderer are identical.

This is all conjectural, yet it coheres.

6

A British God

Merlin reappears in romance, and later, as a vastly elaborated version of the prophet who confounds Vortigern and masterminds the conception of Arthur. He is more complex, more inscrutable, with an air of having antecedents that no one else has. As he develops he seems to embody Something Else, something radically Other, whether or not we detect a god in him.

C.S. Lewis's novel *That Hideous Strength*, the third part of his *Cosmic Trilogy*, leads up to Merlin's reawakening in modern times after a long sleep. Before that event, one of the characters, Dr Dimble, discusses him as the romancers portray him. Dimble recognises, and approves, the medieval Christian antithesis of good and evil, which seems to rule out any sympathy towards Merlin's paternal incubus-demon, and to condemn magic in general as a forbidden art. Yet Merlin, as depicted by medieval Christian authors, apparently puts a query over this view of things. Or perhaps he transcends the antithesis entirely; perhaps, in some strange way, he is prior to it.

Has it ever struck you what an odd creation Merlin is? He's not evil; yet he's a magician. He is obviously a druid; yet he knows all about the Grail. He's 'the devil's son'; but then Layamon goes out of his way to tell you that the kind of being who fathered Merlin needn't have been bad after all. You remember, 'There dwell in the sky many kinds of wights. Some of them are good, and some work evil.'

'I often wonder,' said Dr. Dimble, 'whether Merlin doesn't represent the last trace of something that became impossible when the only people in touch with the supernatural were either white or black, either priests or sorcerers.'

Without necessarily accepting the either/or as Dimble states it, we can agree that the Merlin of medieval romance, appearing after a gap of silence, does seem to have it both ways.

To some extent his ambivalence could be a long-term survival of Celtic Christianity. In Britain and Ireland during the time of conversion Christians were not persecuted by pagan authorities as their continental brethren were – in Britain barely, in Ireland not at all – and they consequently had a less hostile attitude to the old religion and its mythology. Gods and goddesses could survive in disguise, sometimes a thin disguise, as kings and queens, saints and enchanters. Some of the ancient mythology itself survived, in poetry and story-telling.

As we saw, Morgen the 'sea-born', ruling her otherworldly Isle of Avalon, was certainly a goddess in her origins. She was a healer, she was a mathematician, she could change her shape and fly over France and Italy. The first two accomplishments might be purely human, but hardly the others, and she has pagan counterparts whose divinity is beyond question. After Geoffrey's *Vita Merlini*, some story-tellers moved Avalon in from the ocean and equated it with Glastonbury in Somerset, or rather with the almost insular hill-cluster cradling it, a place with otherworldly attributes in its own right, and it became the burial-place of Arthur – in other words, the terminus of his last journey, and therefore the real Avalon. He was said to have been brought there for healing because the lady of the place, Morgan as her name was now spelt, was a cousin of his. Even so, Giraldus Cambrensis (the same who described and defended the Welsh seers) accused the credulous Britons of making her a goddess; and in the later romance *Sir Gawain and the Green Knight*, she is definitely divine again: 'Morgan the Goddess / Rightly is her name' (ll. 2452–3).

Other cases could easily be cited, such as Geoffrey's Belinus and Brennius, the British kings who capture Rome in the *History*. Originally gods, and important ones, they were demoted, they were not anathematised or abolished. Morgen herself was demoted, becoming Arthur's ambiguous and disturbing half-sister Morgan le Fay, but she too survived.

However, no mere reminiscence of survival could account for what Merlin becomes in a Christian literary milieu that is in principle adverse to him: the supreme prophet, the supreme magician, the superhuman and omniscient sponsor of Arthur's Britain. While basically he is still the Merlinus Ambrosius of the *History*, without the Caledonian offshoot, he is not merely Ambrosius.

We might find a clue to the divine being who, on his own testimony, possesses him, by looking at one or more of the aspects that Dimble enumerates. This could, conceivably, lead to a god attested in other contexts. To find an actual name might be too much to hope for. It could be a question of discovering a god outside Britain, probably in the Classical pantheon, with a British counterpart whose 'enclosure' or *temenos* could have been the island of Britain.

Classical authors have a frustrating habit of referring to foreign deities not by their real names, which might be interesting, but by the names of Classical deities they are supposed to be equivalent to. It is irritating to be told that Indians worship Dionysos and Heracles, when the Indian gods concerned turn out to be Siva and Krishna. Still, such obstacles *can* be surmounted if there seems to be light showing on the other side.

Lewis's Dr Dimble says Merlin is 'obviously' a Druid. The implication is that his prophetic powers, and perhaps his magic, have visible antecedents in Druidism and might be illuminated from that source.

Not much is known about the Druids, though plenty is known of the assertions made about them. During the last centuries BC, they flourished among the Celtic peoples of western Europe as an inter-tribal order, active in Gaul, Britain and Ireland. Julius Caesar records that Druidism was systematised among the Britons and its advanced colleges were in the island. His testimony to Britain's pre-eminence carries weight; he is not a weaver of fantasies like some Druid enthusiasts.

Caesar and a few other Classical authors built up a picture of Druidism that remained more or less standard, and had at least some resemblance to reality. Druids appear to have had a variety of functions, magical, bardic, judicial, medical and mediumistic. They advised rulers and had the reputation, rightly or wrongly, of being so influential that they could stop inter-tribal wars. Women could be Druids, but only men could aspire to the higher levels.

Becoming a Druid was understood to require years of study, years spent in sacred caves and wild forest sanctuaries. Study of what? Since Druids seldom wrote anything down, the question is hard to answer. However, Druid lore included astronomy, and had something to do with the calendar. Druids harmonised the solar and lunar years by a nineteen-year cycle, invented in Greece, and decipherable from an inscribed plate called the Coligny Calendar that was found near Bourg-en-Bresse in the French department of Ain. What else Druids were expected to know remained obscure to outsiders, and in spite of the wide range of expertise that their social status demanded there may not have been any official curriculum for all. As for their gods, very little indeed is known about them. Caesar mentions six, and in true Roman fashion gives them Roman names – Mercury, Mars and so forth – with the result that his readers are not much the wiser. Initiated Druids could find their way through the theological maze by personal communion, and give counsel through inspired divination.

Some of this is bringing us close to shamanism, as practised in central Asia and diffused outside. The Druid's ancestor is perhaps the medicine-man, dancing and drumming in ritual gear and conversing with spirits in a self-induced ecstasy. An Irish legend tells of a Druid named Mog Ruith who dressed in a bird outfit, assembled magical equipment and rose into the air – a shamanic spectacle, including the levitation. But shamanism, in its more sophisticated forms, is not merely incantatory spell-binding. The professional shaman, male or female, has undergone a long preparation, is wiser than most of the tribe, and deservedly enjoys its respect. To associate Druidism with shamanism is not necessarily to lower it.

However, the features of the system that stood out for Classical writers were not shamanic. One was the pervasiveness of ritual. The Druids had procedures and ceremonies for everything, and above all for dealing with the gods, through rituals rather than ecstasies. Oak trees were especially important, and the actual word 'Druid' may mean 'oak-knower'. A ritual that attracted particular attention involved mistletoe. When the parasite grew on an oak (which it seldom does), worshippers congregated on the sixth day of the moon, and a Druid cut off a sprig with a golden sickle. He sacrificed two white bulls and everybody feasted.

A more arresting feature of Druidism was a firm belief in life after death, for everybody. This made Celtic warriors exceptionally brave. It attracted interest among Greeks and Romans, who had no such belief. Apart from a few who had been initiated into elite cults like the Eleusinian Mysteries, their dead were usually consigned to perpetual nullity as shades. Greeks thought the Druids believed in reincarnation. This was probably a misunderstanding, owing to the fact that the philosopher Pythagoras was one of the few in the Hellenic world who taught it, and because of his eminence it was the only kind of immortality that Greeks could imagine. Celts, however, went on to another life quite like the present one, on an island or inside a hill. Confidence in the future was so deep-rooted that they could borrow money on an IOU payable in the next life.

The Druid activity that overshadowed all others was the practice of ritual sacrifice, not only of animals but of human beings. It was performed in wooden shrines and forest sanctuaries. Victims were stabbed, or shot at with arrows, or drowned in tubs, or burned in wicker cages. This was a kind of religion that aroused the enmity of the Romans, who condemned Druidism as subversive anyway. They outlawed human sacrifice wherever their authority spread.

Thus far, no reason emerges why Lewis, or the character in his novel, should speak of Merlin as a Druid or expect Druidism to shed light on him. There are shamanistic traits in the early Merlin, with his controlling spirit and his prophetic ecstasy, but not in the later manifestations, and in any case Druidic shamanism is not conspicuous enough as a clue. The boyhood story of Merlin nearly being sacrificed is interesting, as showing that a tradition of the practice survived long after its abolition. Vortigern's magicians may be Druids, and in one manuscript they are called so. But Merlin has no notion of performing a sacrifice himself.

When the Romans reached the Menai Strait, and prepared to cross it to extirpate Druidism in Anglesey, they saw an alarming spectacle on the other side, as recorded in Tacitus:

> Drawn up on the seashore was a dense mass of armed warriors. Among them, bearing flaming torches, ran women with funereal robes and dishevelled hair like Furies, and all around stood Druids, raising their hands to heaven and calling down dreadful curses.

It is hard to picture Merlin in that sort of company.

C.S. Lewis, however, did not have to try. When he counted Merlin as a Druid, he was showing awareness of a conception of Druidism that would fit Merlin more appropriately: a glorified conception, for which Greek authors were responsible. The original culprits lived in Alexandria, a highly cultured and cosmopolitan city. Like many other sophisticated people, these Greeks reacted against the civilisation around them, and cherished nostalgia for the lost golden age of Classical myth. They wanted to believe that there might, somewhere beyond civilisation's frontiers, be human societies that had not lost this glorious past. Theirs was a theory of the 'Noble Savage' type, propagated by Rousseau many centuries later, except that the people whom these dreamers imagined were by no means savages. They were pacific and philosophic, dedicated to wisdom and spirituality, and probably to vegetarianism. The Celts of north-western Europe could be romanticised in this way because they were still unfamiliar enough to romanticise. So their Druids could be interpreted, from a distance, as home-grown sages and philosopher-statesmen. The Druids' doctrine of immortality, however misunderstood, allowed the Alexandrians to believe that they had learned from Pythagoras. Nor did speculation stop there. Early in the Christian era it began to be asserted that the truth was the other way round. Pythagoras had not taught the Druids, the Druids had taught Pythagoras. And since the Druids' principal colleges were in Britain, the role of Britain might be special.

The notion of a primordial British Wisdom proved to have a stubborn vitality, with or without Druids. Milton took it up in *Areopagitica*: 'Writers of good antiquity and ablest judgment have been perswaded that ev'n the school of Pythagoras, and the Persian wisdom took beginning from the old Philosophy of this Iland.' During the eighteenth century, societies were formed to revive the 'old Philosophy'. It was because of this trend that antiquaries such as Stukeley were able to launch the too-durable illusion that the Druids built Stonehenge.

The notion of a wise and virtuous northern region, including Britain, was associated with another nation besides the Druid-enlightened Celts, though, eventually, the wishful fantasies overlapped. These more mysterious Utopians were the Hyperboreans, or 'dwellers-at-the-back-of-the-North-Wind', whose homeland was presumably tranquil and temperate. Convergent traditions in Asia as well as Europe suggest that there was a real Hyperborean nation in north-central Asia, and that it was the home of a form of shamanism, which spread direct and indirect influence over a wide area through wandering practitioners. Pythagoras met a Hyperborean sage named Abaris who has been claimed, quite seriously, as a shaman.

The Hyperboreans were supposed to have a special affinity with one of the greatest of the Greek gods, Apollo. They were said to have played a part in establishing his oracular shrine at Delphi, and he was absent from it for three months each year, during which time he visited his Hyperborean friends, travelling through the sky in a flying chariot.

With the passage of time the Hyperboreans became vague. A priest of Apollo, Aristeas, had made a journey of exploration through central Asia which probably did show where the Hyperboreans actually lived, so far as they existed at all. But Aristeas's journey was forgotten, and the Hyperboreans' homeland was shifted across Russia into Europe, until they were being blended with Celts, and their divine wisdom was both Hyperborean and Druidic.

In Classical times the Hyperboreans' friend Apollo was one of the most characteristically Greek of the gods. He was a divine patron of music, mathematics and healing. According to legend Pythagoras was his son. But he was not, in his origins, entirely Greek. He came from outside, with his sister Artemis (otherwise Diana), and planted himself at Delphi by ousting a senior occupant. His Asian connection was not fictitious. He (or a prior deity that went into his making) probably had shamanic roots.

As a spiritual heir of Asian prophets, he became, supremely, the god of prophecy himself.

He acquired several oracular shrines, Delphi, however, being always the greatest, so sacred that it was the only centre of unity among the Greek city-states. Governments consulted it as a matter of normal policy, and employed professional interpreters to explain the messages they received. Individual consultations were allowed, but they were expensive, and confined to a single day each month. Inside the precinct Apollo's priestesses, intoxicated by fumes, poured out what were supposed to be god-dictated communications. Priests interpreted these, sometimes in verse. While Apollo's responses were usually given as advice, some had a predictive aspect, though the prediction might be taken in different ways, and Apollo had the nickname Loxias, the Ambiguous.

He also inspired unattached persons, mostly women, and with them he could be worse than ambiguous. According to legend, he conferred prophetic powers on Cassandra in return for sexual favours, and then, when she changed her mind, ordained that while she could go on prophesying, no one would believe her. Despite her unhappy experience, Giraldus Cambrensis, defending the mantic frenzies of the Welsh prophets, cited Cassandra without questioning that her gift was valid. Apollo also imparted it on a more regular basis to freelance prophetesses called Sibyls. One, who lived in a cave at Cumae near Naples, was treated with profound respect; she figures in Virgil's *Aeneid*. 'Sibylline books' were kept in Rome and consulted in times of crisis. Michelangelo painted Sibyls in the Sistine Chapel because it was believed that some had foretold Christ, and therefore they counted as honorary Christians.

One document of the Hyperborean *mélange* takes us unequivocally to Britain, and to a god who could be the conjectural key to Merlin.

Greeks founding colonies overseas invoked Apollo as their patron, and built temples for him in their new settlements. But Hecataeus of Abdera, in the fourth century BC, ranges further afield. He informs his readers that Hyperboreans live in Britain, and that the island is a dwelling-place for a being whom he identifies as Apollo. Here are some extracts from what he says, as quoted by the historian Diodorus*:

> Opposite to the coast of Celtic Gaul there is an island in the ocean, not smaller than Sicily, and lying to the north – which is inhabited by the Hyperboreans.

The island is obviously Britain, still unfamiliar to Greeks in Hecataeus's time. Apollo's Hyperborean friends, after a literary drift westward, have come to rest as its people.

> Tradition says that Latona [Apollo's mother, otherwise Leto] was born there, and for that reason the inhabitants venerate Apollo more than any other god. . . .
>   In this island, there is a magnificent precinct of Apollo, and a remarkable temple, of a round form.

This temple is surely Stonehenge, and many readers have taken that for granted, but it is necessary in fairness to point out a difficulty. The word translated 'round' does not, strictly

* See Robert Graves's translation in *The White Goddess* (London: Faber & Faber, 1952), pp. 283–4.

speaking, mean 'circular', it means 'spherical'. Since a spherical temple is impossible, it is likely that Hecataeus, learning of the island by hearsay, has used inexact language and 'circular' is the meaning. There is no alternative candidate. If Stonehenge is allowed, we have an immediate Myrddin link via the sacred bluestones that formed the primary circle.

> There is also a city, sacred to the same god, most of the inhabitants of which are harpers.

One city. Moridunum, otherwise Carmarthen?

> The Hyperboreans use a peculiar dialect, and have a remarkable attachment to the Greeks. . . . It is also said that in this island the moon appears very near the earth, that certain eminences of a terrestrial form are plainly seen on it, and that Apollo visits the island once in a course of nineteen years, in which period the stars complete their revolutions. During the season of his appearance the god plays upon the harp and dances every night.

Did the Britons invent telescopes and see the lunar mountains? However that may be, the references to the nineteen-year cycle, by which the Druids regulated their calendar, shows further what company we may be in, and this account of Apollo's visits is not taken from Greek mythology, which makes his personal trips to Hyperborean country more frequent.

It would be going too far to suggest that the god with a home in Britain actually *is* Apollo. There are few signs that he made his way to the island before Roman imperialism carried him there. Here as elsewhere, we are probably witnessing the use of a classically familiar name for an analogous deity worshipped among a foreign people, perhaps with some kind of calendar-regulated festival. But if Hecataeus is talking of a British god who can be credibly identified with Apollo, that god is presumably a source of divine prophecy – and so the divine Myrddin is.

In the Roman period at least, when the great Apollo came to be known in Britain, a British god actually was identified with him – or, at least, was seen as a Celtic aspect of him, not merely in speculation but in cultic practice. He was Maponus, the 'Divine Youth'. Five inscriptions in Britain attest the identification. One reason for it may have been musical. An inscription at Hexham equates Maponus with 'Apollo the Harper'. Hecataeus shows the same notion at work. The inscriptions are in Northumbria, Cumbria and Lancashire. Maponus's northern worship is also reflected in the Scottish village named Lochmaben, and in a megalith, Clochmabenstane. But the cult is recorded on the continent, and a seventh-century geographer at Ravenna in Italy notes a place in Britain called the Locus Maponi, though without telling where it is.

Maponus may not seem important enough to carry much weight, but a British Apollo who was overshadowed and assimilated by the imperial pantheon may have been more prominent before. While the known traces of his actual worship are northern, he metamorphoses in Wales, as other British gods do, and becomes a mythical character called Mabon. As such, he is involved in various adventures, including an episode of *Culhwch and Olwen* which is crucial to Culhwch's success. He even appears in continental Arthurian romances, his name only slightly altered.

The most significant thing in all this is the way he is designated. He is 'Mabon son of Modron', meaning 'Son, son of

Mother', a most peculiar way of defining a male person, who, in Welsh, would normally be bracketed with his father. Modron is doubtless the Mother Goddess. Rachel Bromwich mentions a text in which 'Mabon' means Christ, who had no earthly father. That is exceptional. What matters with Mabon is the Merlin connection. The Divine Youth is, precisely, the boy-without-a-father who is sought for and found in a human manifestation at Carmarthen, where he should be, as He-of-Moridunum.

In Maponus we may, just may, be getting a glimpse of the being who appears in Geoffrey of Monmouth as a 'controlling spirit'. In the context of twelfth-century Christianity, he cannot be openly divine. Yet it is surprising to find who *could* be openly divine, even then, if the divinity had a respectable literary background. In an early chapter of Geoffrey's *History*, when Brutus and his followers are wandering through the Mediterranean, he seeks and obtains guidance at a deserted temple, where he is told in a dream to head for a far-away island in the ocean. His prayer is framed in correct elegiac couplets, and so is the reply. The speaker of the reply, who sets the Trojans on course for their exalted destiny, is the 'living goddess' Diana, otherwise Artemis, Apollo's sister. They settle in their promised new home, renamed 'Britain' after their leader, and found the city of New Troy beside the Thames. It has only one major temple – only one that is mentioned, anyhow – and this is a temple of Apollo himself.

Whatever the echoes of tradition, it would be detracting from the British god to make him simply an insular echo of a more famous Mediterranean one. If he was truly as conjectured, he would have been a tutelary spirit of the island in his own right, the Myrddin-god empowering other Myrddins. Apollo gradually faded out after the triumph of Christianity, whereas

Myrddin continued, as some other Celtic deities did. He was still a presence well into the Christian era, in Ambrosius, in Lailoken, in Ganieda.

The *White Book* allusion to early Britain as his 'precinct' or *temenos* supplies a name that may be put in its better-known form, Merlin. The imaginative archaeologist T.C. Lethbridge once wrote a series of studies entitled *Merlin's Island*. He knew what he was talking about. If the *White Book* is any guide, Britain was the domain of an ancestral deity who may be called Merlin, and the island was his island.

Dinas Emrys hillfort, Gwynedd. (*Janet & Colin Bord/Fortean Picture Library*)

Bardsey Island, Gwynedd. (*Janet & Colin Bord/Fortean Picture Library*)

Illustration of Merlin and his mother by
Miranda Gray, from Rowley's *The Birth of
Merlin*, edited by R.J. Stewart.

Merlin's Mount, Marlborough, Wiltshire.
(Fortean Picture Library)

Gustave Doré's engraving depicting Arthur being found on the beach by Merlin. *(Mary Evans Picture Library)*

Tintagel Castle, Cornwall. (*Janet & Colin Bord/Fortean Picture Library*)

'King Arthur's Round Table', Winchester. (*Janet & Colin Bord/Fortean Picture Library*)

Merlin in his study. *(Wessex Books)*

Vortigern and the dragons.
(Wessex Books)

Merlin building Stonehenge.
(Wessex Books)

Merlin and Vivien at rest under a
tree. *(Many Evans Picture Library)*

Merlin and a present-day boy whom he befriends, from *Merlin Awakes*, Graham Howells/ Pont Books, Gomer Press.

The chateau of Comper-en-Broceliande, associated with Merlin and Vivien. (*Wessex Books*)

Chalice Orchard, Glastonbury. *(Photo by Patricia Ashe)*

Merlin's tomb in the Forest of Paimpont, Brittany. *(Janet & Colin Bord/Fortean Picture Library)*

7

MERLiN AND The GRAiL

Medieval Europe recognised three main sources of imaginative literature: the Matter of Rome, the Matter of France and the Matter of Britain. The first meant Classical antiquity, Greek as well as Roman. The second meant the heroic cycle of the Emperor Charlemagne and his peers, the chief of them being Roland, who fell at Roncesvalles. The third meant the constellation of traditions and legends around King Arthur. To some extent, the third was a consequence of the second and a retort to it, with political overtones. The kings of France boasted an illustrious pedigree going back to Charlemagne himself. Thanks to Geoffrey of Monmouth, the kings of England, by comparison a parvenu dynasty, were enabled to claim a more illustrious pedigree going back to Arthur.

However, Arthurian romance became an international phenomenon in several languages, ranging far outside even quasi-history. It was the favourite form of imaginative fiction, with something in it for everyone: love, tournaments, wars, dragon-slaying, magic, religion. During the later twelfth century interests in general were broadening, and there were more people than hitherto whose literary tastes carried weight – in particular, more women. The multiplying manuscripts were not meant for the solitary reader, they were for groups, with literate members reading the text aloud.

After the Norman conquest of England, western France and England were dominated by a French-speaking nobility, and alongside the English kings' continental empire were the domains of the French kings. Geoffrey's Arthurian story was disseminated through a large aristocratic public by Wace's French paraphrase. Arthurian romances in verse and prose were probably being written to entertain this public before any that have survived. The genre was established in the 1160s by Chrétien de Troyes. Very little is known about him beyond what can be inferred from his dedications, notably one to Marie de Champagne, a daughter of Louis VII and Eleanor of Aquitaine. He certainly enjoyed aristocratic patronage. A gifted poet, he transformed the atmosphere and personnel of the legends, introducing (for instance) Sir Lancelot and his love for the queen, and the first known mention of Camelot. He almost detached the Matter of Britain from history, even quasi-history. With some of the romancers who followed, the break was not quite so total, but the trend was towards totality, and Arthur's Britain became a sort of chivalric Utopia, governed by courtly ideals which Arthur's knights professed, if they did not always live up to them. Chrétien launched the mystique of the Holy Grail, which was instrumental in Merlin's return. However, he never mentions him. The return was the achievement of a lesser but extremely inventive poet, Robert de Boron, who flourished around 1200.

＋・ ⚔ ・＋

Robert de Boron played a significant part in the growth of Arthurian romance. On the specific issue of reintroducing Merlin, he faced an immediate problem: how to explain who he was and where he came from. As we saw, Christianity was, so to speak, hardening, becoming more black-and-white, leaving Celtic ambiguities further and further behind. In story-telling the benign goddess Morgen, the lady of Avalon, was on her way to becoming a sorceress. It was harder than it had been to envisage the possibility of a 'good' seer or enchanter, when such activities were usually condemned as forbidden. Moreover, there was a special difficulty with the odd being who took the place of a father in Merlin's conception. Ostensibly the incubus had to be evil. Yet Robert was determined that the son should be good. He solved the problem boldly by dismissing Geoffrey's neutral demon and substituting a frankly diabolic agent, in keeping with Christian convention, but then sidestepping the consequences.

He pictures a conclave of devils complaining of the triumph of Christianity, and trying to counter-attack by creating a human champion of their own, to oppose Christ with supernatural powers. One of them craftily impregnates a woman without her knowing. However, the scheme is thwarted by her virtue and innocence. Her son Merlin has none of the intended anti-Christian malice, but he keeps the supernatural gifts which the devil has instilled and has no way of cancelling. In particular, he has a boundless knowledge of things past, present and future.

There is even more to him than that. He is hardly a human being at all in the normal sense, but a hybrid justifying the puzzlement of Dr Dimble in C.S. Lewis's novel. Recalling Geoffrey's hints that Merlin grew up quickly, Robert takes that idea further into sheer fairy-tale. His Merlin is talking eloquently before he is 3 years old. He asks Blaise, his mother's confessor, to keep a record, a sort of journal; this purports to be the basis of Robert's narrative. When the prodigy is 7, Robert goes on to what is substantially Geoffrey's story of Vortigern, with the tower, the dragons, and so forth, but in a very different spirit. The roles of the participants (including the dragons) are changed, and everything is spun out longer, with much talk and copious detail.

Merlin goes on growing and is now unequivocally a magician. He is still the builder of Stonehenge, but now he does it by magic. He still aids the sons of Constantine, but now by bewildering feats of foresight and shape-shifting. You never know when an ordinary-looking herdsman or woodcutter will turn out to be Merlin. In anthropological jargon he is a Trickster. The Uther-Ygerna encounter takes far more arranging, and has unexpected touches of realism: Merlin and the third man accompany Uther into Ygerna's bedroom and pull his boots off for him. Robert, unlike Geoffrey, makes it clear that Merlin is preparing the way for Arthur's reign from the beginning. When the child is born, he takes him away and leaves him in the care of a foster-father for safety. No one else, not even the foster-father, is to know who he is till the time comes for his accession. His fostering becomes a permanent feature of Merlin's legend.

When King Uther dies, apparently without an heir, Geoffrey's quasi-history is left behind. Robert introduces the famous test that establishes Arthur's right to be king, as Uther's son and successor. Merlin reappears and calls together the principal lords. He tells them to assemble at Christmas and pray for an upright king who will champion Christianity; they will be given a sign. It is not clear what authority Merlin has, but they assemble without argument. When they are all together in a church, a great square block of stone materialises outside the building, with an anvil on top and a sword thrust down through it into the stone. According to an inscription on the sword, whoever can draw it out will be king by divine election. Many men try, unsuccessfully, but the boy Arthur, who has come with his guardian, does it without trouble. Since he is unknown and obscure, there is great reluctance to acknowledge him. However, Merlin, who has stayed in the background during the unsuccessful attempts, now proclaims Arthur's true paternity.

The king still has fighting to do until his position is secure. Merlin helps him as he helped Uther. Robert has laid the groundwork for fantastic events, and these, as told by other romancers besides himself, begin to happen.

One of Geoffrey's neglected threads is belatedly picked up. Arthur's wonderful sword is Caliburn, later Excalibur. The name is probably derived from *chalybs*, the Latin for steel. In the best-known account of its acquisition, it is not (as modern readers are apt to imagine) the sword extracted from the stone, but a replacement. Arthur breaks the first sword in combat. Merlin promises to get him a new one and conducts him to an unidentified lake, where he sees an arm rising above the surface, with a sheathed sword grasped in its hand. The Lady of the Lake approaches and bestows her blessing. Arthur rows out and takes the sword: Excalibur. It will be his till his reign ends and it must be returned to the lake. Merlin tells him to value the scabbard too, more than the sword, if anything. So long as he has it, he will be protected from injury.

The motif of the weapon in water cannot be rationalised, but it may be a remote echo of ancient custom. Peat bogs in Denmark are the silted-up remnants of pools where swords were sunk a long time ago, sometimes with rocks holding them down, or with the tips of their blades bent. A warrior's sword was virtually an extension of himself, and it might be submerged after his death, having been made useless for anyone else.

The Lady of the Lake is a survivor from the pre-Christian world, like Morgen, and like Morgen she presides over a sisterhood. Several Damsels of the Lake are her companions in an enchanted subaqueous abode, though they are free to leave it and go about in the world when they feel inclined. The Lady is not an individual with a permanent title but the head of the sisterhood at any particular time, and the holder of that position may retire or die. At least four names are mentioned by various authors, including Nimue and Viviane. The Lady and her companions are generally friendly to Arthur. One of them, however, is fatal to Merlin.

As the monarch whom Merlin has enthroned, Arthur is wise and just and generous. But the story-tellers' preoccupation with the adventures and love-affairs of the knights around him tends to make him less dominant himself. He is not the towering leader of Geoffrey's *History* but a magnificent chairman. As for his humbler subjects, very little is said about them, or about his style of government.

The kingdom has no intelligible structure, and no convincing map can be drawn. It has not even, properly speaking, a capital. Camelot is Arthur's personal headquarters. No one reigns there before or after him; according to two accounts the malignant Cornish king Mark destroyed it when he was gone. Vaguely located in southern England, Camelot is a splendid dream-city, a point of arrival and departure, the centre of the Arthurian universe. It is a source of inspiration, and it has a religious aura. Several knights go there for baptism.

As Arthur's headquarters Camelot may be linked by a long thread of tradition to the headquarters of an actual British king, from whom his legend originated. It is here that the special status of Cadbury Castle in Somerset – which can be traced at least to the thirteenth century in a map in Hereford Cathedral – may be relevant. Cadbury is an Iron Age hill-fort that was captured and cleared of inhabitants by the Romans, but reoccupied in the second half of the fifth century by an overlord – king or military leader – with great resources of manpower, who refortified it on an unparalleled scale, with touches of architectural sophistication not found in other British hill-forts.

Whatever its antecedents, King Arthur's Camelot, the Camelot of romance, is the focus of his noble order of knights, and houses the Round Table where they assemble. The Table first appears in Wace, but romance makes it a creation of Merlin, with a new character and symbolism. The change may have been precipitated by sheer practical logic, when the first conception became unworkable. Wace gives the common-sense reason for it: that its shape prevented disputes over precedence, because all the knights seated at it were equal.

However, this is not an adequate reason. The king has to sit somewhere, and whoever is next to him, close enough to talk, will be more important than the occupants of other places. Also, when the knights were few, the table could be of a practicable size, but it ceased to be so with the enrolment of more and more. In the fifteenth-century version by Sir Thomas Malory there are 140 or 150. Contemporary illustrators are aware of the difficulties. Some convert the Table from a disc to a ring, with gaps for servitors to pass through; it would still need a very big hall to house it, and conversation across the void would be impossible. Other artists imply that the knights don't all sit down at the same time. As for the problem over proximity to the king, a German picture shows Arthur in the centre of the disc, equidistant from every seat. How did he get there? Did he crawl underneath and come up through a hole? And even that would not work, because the knights whom he faced would be more important than the ones behind his back, and to preserve impartiality he would have to sit on a swivel chair and rotate.

The absurdity of the all-equal Table might not, in itself, have caused Merlin's revaluation of the furniture. But the revaluation happens, and is very serious indeed. It has its place in the greatest and most mystifying of Arthurian themes, which makes the Matter of Britain different from all other bodies of romance: the Grail.

There is nothing mysterious about the word itself. In medieval French a *graal* was simply a large serving-dish or bowl. In the first of the Grail stories, a long but unfinished poem by Chrétien, a young wanderer named Perceval comes to an isolated castle and is welcomed by its lord, who is known as the Fisher King. He is incapacitated by a wound. Perceval sees a strange procession pass through the hall, in which the principal figure is a maiden carrying a graal in her hands. The graal is 'worked with fine gold' and ornamented with beautiful jewels. Clearly this is something more than an item of tableware, and it transpires that Perceval could heal the Fisher King by asking about it, but he keeps silent and the spell is not broken. Later, Chrétien says that an 'old king' living in an adjacent room is kept alive by a single Mass wafer brought to him regularly in the graal, and the vessel itself is holy; but in the surviving text, the poet still does not reveal what it is, or what its holiness consists in.

Further developments come with other authors. The object is presented as *the* graal or Grail, a particular sacred vessel. The conception is Christian, but the mystique surrounding the Grail draws in elements from pagan myth, especially myths about food-producing vessels such as magic cauldrons and horns of plenty. The Grail is a source of nourishment, as it is for the unseen dweller in the castle, and while the nourishment becomes spiritual, the material aspect never vanishes altogether.

The usual explanation of what the Grail is comes from Robert de Boron, who combines it with his account of Merlin. The Grail is the vessel of the Last Supper in which Christ instituted the sacrament. This cup or dish would hardly have been 'worked with fine gold' or ornamented with jewels, but Robert ignores the objection. He gives it a long early history, based on the New Testament and in part on apocryphal Christian books.

Joseph of Arimathea, he says, obtained the Grail, which he used to catch drops of Christ's blood after the crucifixion, and later supplied his tomb. Joseph was imprisoned by hostile Jews. Christ appeared to him, returned the Grail to his hands, and taught him 'secret words' to be uttered in conjunction with it, which were the key to a special revelation about the Trinity. After a long imprisonment Joseph was released. He assembled a number of kinsfolk and disciples, and formed a community. They received divine messages through the Grail, and made a table on which to keep it; this table commemorated the table of the Last Supper. Joseph's brother-in-law Bron caught a fish and placed it on the table. He was the first to be called the Rich Fisher or the Fisher King. He had a son, Alain, who would eventually be the Grail's custodian himself.

In response to divine commands, Bron, Alain, and other members of the community took the Grail to Britain, specifically to the 'vales of Avalon', the future site of Glastonbury. Joseph did not accompany them. Other stories were to bring him to Britain in person, and make him the founder of Christian Glastonbury.

Then there is a hiatus. The Grail seems to be removed elsewhere, and to pass to keepers collaterally descended from Joseph. Its whereabouts become obscure. Robert overleaps a long interval and describes Merlin reporting all this to King Uther, showing how the Grail gives Britain a unique status in Christendom. He tells Uther to have a third table made, in succession to the other two, completing the symbolism of the Trinity. Another author makes it symbolic also of the round Earth and the heavens. It is, of course, the Round Table itself at which Arthur's knights will be seated, or some of them, the principal members of the order; the idea of accommodating them all is abandoned. Merlin tells Uther that one place at the table must be kept vacant. This is called the Perilous Seat, and can only be occupied with impunity by the knight who will succeed in the Grail Quest which Merlin foresees when Arthur is king.

The Quest motif is very ancient, and in an early Welsh poem attributed (wrongly) to Taliesin, Arthur and his companions actually undertake one, their goal being a magic cauldron in a kind of Otherworld – a pagan anticipation of the Grail itself. The Quest anticipated by Merlin is more than a hunt for a lost object. Its aim is not merely to locate the Grail, which is never regarded as a tangible holy relic like other holy relics. The Church, as a matter of fact, never took any notice of it, and Glastonbury Abbey, which claimed other relics by the hundred, never claimed this one.

In its most exalted form, the Quest of the Grail is related to the belief in Christ's presence in the sacrament. It might be inferred that the Grail in which he instituted the sacrament must have a unique sanctity and spiritual power. 'Achieving' the Grail (in the end, only the saintly Galahad does) appears to mean looking inside it and undergoing a supreme spiritual experience, hinted at in Christ's 'secret words' to Joseph – a vision unfolding the mystery of the Trinity, and the incarnation of its Second Person in Christ. It is the same vision that Dante imagines at the close of the *Divine Comedy*.

◆━ ═◆═ ━◆

The Quest, however, does not happen in Merlin's time. Before it, he disappears again, unexpectedly and shockingly.

In view of his bizarre nature, it might be guessed that he would be a stranger to sexual relations. No woman is mentioned in that connection till he is middle-aged. Then, however, the lightning strikes. He becomes hopelessly enamoured of one of the Damsels of the Lake, Nimue or Viviane. While he knows, of course, that this love will be disastrous, he cannot avert his doom. She rejects his advances, but, having extracted a promise that he will not use magic to overcome her resistance, she agrees to accompany him on a long tour of Brittany and Cornwall, and learns much secret lore on the way. She is fully aware of his being the son of a devil. At last, tired of his persistence, she uses one of his own spells to immure him in a magical prison. Accounts of its nature vary. It may be a cave or tomb, or, in a kindlier version, a pleasant enclosure with invisible walls, where she visits him but never releases him. It may be in Cornwall, or in the enchanted Breton forest of Broceliande, where Wace failed to see fairies.

This depressing story may have been inspired by plain anti-feminism. As Chaucer's Wife of Bath shows in her Prologue, the Middle Ages produced plenty of literature hostile to women. Or it may be a result of the same tightening of Christian attitudes that denigrated Morgen. Romancers possibly felt that a magician, however great his achievement, however supportive he might be of Christianity, could not be truly good or permanently approved by heaven. So Merlin's equivocal nature had to carry the sense of a nemesis, a betrayal through his own arts, and it was only proper that his downfall should be catastrophic and shameful. It certainly is.

When Merlin is lost to Arthur, his tutelary power is withdrawn. It does not seem so immediately. The kingdom continues to flourish. An apparition of the Grail (veiled, however, from direct sight) hovers one day over the Round Table when the principal knights are seated at it. An interesting detail is that the vessel's ancestral pre-Christian quality still clings to it: each knight feels that he is receiving the food of his choice. Galahad has proved that he can occupy the Perilous Seat, and many others vow to go on the Quest. Arthur is unhappy at this. The Grail-seekers are deserting their posts, and he foresees that some will never return.

The Quest goes on for a long time. A few of the knights have glimpses, but only Galahad, confronting the Grail at last in a foreign land, attains the full vision . . . and dies in ecstasy. Arthur's forebodings turn out to be correct. Many of the seekers are lost to him, and the Order is attenuated. The losses can be made up by recruitment, but disaster is approaching. Modred, Arthur's nephew (or, according to rumour, his illicitly begotten son), is plotting against him. Lancelot and the queen are lovers, as they have been for some time, and Arthur has been turning a blind eye. Modred forces the scandal into the open. The king is compelled to condemn his wife to death. Lancelot rescues her, but the Round Table is divided between his supporters and the

king's. Soon we are back, more or less, with Geoffrey of
Monmouth. Modred makes his bid for the crown, the final
battle virtually wipes out the knighthood, and the wounded
Arthur is taken away over the water to Avalon.

Several of the major developments, such as Merlin's
incarceration, the Grail Quest and the last exterminatory
conflict, are accepted Arthurian orthodoxy. In English-speaking
countries this is mainly because of the great fifteenth-century
work by Sir Thomas Malory, which adapts older material but is
a masterpiece in its own right. However, the earlier Robert de
Boron has a different and quieter ending that may be preferred,
even though it is lacking in high tragedy. The final battle takes
place, but Arthur assures the Britons that he will not die of his
wound, and his return is seriously expected. The Grail is safely
in the keeping of Perceval, who has become the custodian, and
Merlin has not been incarcerated. He bids farewell to his friends
and explains that Christ does not wish him to appear to people
again, but he will live in happiness till the end of the world. He
makes himself a hermitage called his *esplumoir*, and vanishes into
it. The word *esplumoir* means 'shedding of feathers', and refers to
a place where birds were kept during moulting. It implies,
figuratively, the casting-off of an old life and the beginning of a
new one.

Merlin's immortality is not further enlarged upon. However,
the Welsh also reject his female entrapment, and make him
immortal, with a retreat on the island of Bardsey – as will
appear.

Note on the Winchester Round Table
and its Implications

During the later Middle Ages a popular form of aristocratic entertainment was the 'Round Table'. Participants dressed up as Arthurian characters, jousted, feasted, danced and so on. The table in Winchester Castle Hall (strictly speaking, the table-top, since the twelve legs are missing) was probably the centre-piece of an entertainment like this and may have been made for Edward I, who presided at several. It is made of oak, is 18 feet across and 2¾ inches thick, and weighs over a ton.

Originally it had no design painted on it, and there was nothing to date it. The chronicler John Hardyng, who mentions it in 1450, seems to have thought it was the real thing, and so did Caxton, Malory's printer. The design on the Table now, which gives it the appearance of a huge dart-board, was painted in 1522 for Henry VIII and repainted without change in 1789. It provides places for a king and twenty-four knights. If they all sat down together, they would be extremely crowded, shoulder to shoulder. An appreciably larger company would be impossible.

8

Spenser's Myth

uring the Middle Ages Italy made no major contributions to the Matter of Britain, as such, or to the Matter of France, as such. Then, soon after Malory, Italian poets abruptly started off in a fresh direction. They combined the two, and invented a literary genre sometimes called the Romantic Epic.

First came Matteo Boiardo, who left a long but unfinished verse romance when he died in 1494. After him came Ludovico Ariosto, who composed a sequel that was, in effect, a new work and a much greater one. Boiardo preserved the traditional framework of the old French *Song of Roland*, an epic that was essentially masculine and martial. His story is about paladins fighting paynims, Christians fighting pagans. It is centred on the Emperor Charlemagne with his Twelve Peers, and the chief hero is Roland.

But with Boiardo and, to a greater degree, Ariosto, the reader is brought much closer to the atmosphere of Arthurian romance. Interest shifts to the exploits of individual knights, and Charlemagne acquires a round table. Roland is Italianised as Orlando; he becomes a lover and is even driven out of his mind by love, because of a woman's faithlessness. Boiardo's poem is entitled *Orlando Innamorato*, Orlando in Love, Ariosto's is *Orlando Furioso*, Orlando Mad. It won an international public.

Romantic epic is full of giants and monsters, sorceresses and Saracens. Ariosto has wonderful anachronisms. His characters include Constantine the Great (died 337), Edward IV of England (died 1483), and the vaguely medieval Asian potentate Prester John. Someone receives messages from Merlin, whose eerie place of confinement is described. A ninth-century army uses cannon. All this is carried along by Ariosto's rare sense of humour, and the rapid movement is aided by his verse-form, the *ottava rima*, adapted to English by Byron in *Don Juan*.

In Ariosto's wake England produced one poetic masterpiece that could qualify as a romantic epic, though there was far more to it than that. Edmund Spenser (*c.* 1552–99), the author of *The Faerie Queene*, had a lofty sense of his responsibilities. He rivalled Ariosto's fertility of invention, but with a moral gravity far removed from the Italian's light-heartedness. His vast allegory is surprising in at least one respect. It is not normally counted as belonging to Arthurian literature, yet it portrays Merlin in a unique role that is extraordinarily interesting.

Spenser began writing while at Pembroke College, Cambridge. He was fortunate enough to become friendly with Sir Philip Sidney and other prominent people having literary interests. An early pastoral work, *The Shepheard's Calender*, dedicated to Sidney, is one of the first notable productions of Elizabethan poetry. In 1580 Spenser was appointed secretary to the Lord Deputy of Ireland, and assisted in repressing Irish rebellion. He was rewarded with Kilcolman Castle in Cork, where he settled in 1586.

Sir Walter Raleigh read three completed books of *The Faerie Queene* and introduced Spenser at the court in London. Back in his Irish castle he remarried, and wrote one of the most beautiful of Elizabethan sonnet sequences, *Amoretti*. A prose essay, *A View of the Present State of Ireland*, is highly imperialist, as is part of *The Faerie Queene* itself, to which he now added three further books. In 1598 Irish insurgents burned Kilcolman Castle. Spenser and his wife escaped to England and settled in London, but he died soon afterwards.

The Faerie Queene is written in nine-line 'Spenserian' stanzas, with a leisurely, sometimes dreamlike, effect. Few things happen quickly. The allegory is complex and interwoven, and focused on Gloriana, the Fairy Queen; she stands (more or less) for Elizabeth I, to whom Spenser dedicated his work with repeated flattery. Knights and other characters at her court typify moral qualities – holiness, temperance, chastity and so forth – and have appropriate adventures. Each of the knights is a central figure in a twelve-canto book. 'Fierce wars and faithful loves,' Spenser declares, 'shall moralise my song.' There is much violence and much love, and, in the spirit of romantic epic, there are dragons, giants, enchanters, witches and villains, together with symbolic figures of various kinds.

While *The Faerie Queene* is admittedly not Arthurian, Arthur enters the stories several times, as a gallant young prince undergoing preparation for his magnificent destiny. He never becomes king, because Spenser never reached that point. His overall project was ambitious, perhaps too ambitious to be practicable. Twelve books with Prince Arthur in them were to have been followed by a sequel showing his virtues as king. Spenser, however, did not finish even the first part. He completed only six books of it, with fragments of a seventh, and none of the sequel. What we have may be hardly more than a quarter of what was intended.

In the existing portion Spenser gives hints and indications of what is to come, and just begins to bring in Arthurian characters such as Sir Tristram. The projected future in the sequel would presumably have covered the ground of Arthurian romance, but none of it is developed. He has a problem here, because, as an ardent supporter of the Tudor Queen, he believes in the Tudor myth, as it has been called. This underlies much of his conception, and in the absence of a second part to express it fully, he has to insinuate it into the first. For that purpose he introduces Merlin, and takes a step back before the romances, into Geoffrey of Monmouth country.

His Fairyland is not simply England in disguise, but it reflects England, and a particular view of the monarchy that was gaining ground for a century before Spenser. In 1485 – the year when Caxton, by an opportune coincidence, published Malory's *Morte d'Arthur* – the Wars of the Roses ended with the triumph of Henry Tudor, who became Henry VII. Though only fractionally a Welshman, he liked to see himself as Welsh, and marched from Wales to oust Richard III under a banner bearing a red dragon. His propagandists claimed that he had an independent right to the crown by descent from Cadwallader, the last 'British' king in Geoffrey's *History*. In the Tudors, King Arthur had, figuratively, returned. Henry had his eldest son baptised at Winchester, which Malory said was Camelot, and named him Arthur so that he could reign as Arthur II. Unhappily the prince died young, and the succession passed to his brother as Henry VIII. The myth did not expire. The antiquary John Leland invoked Geoffrey of Monmouth and hailed Henry as 'Arturius Redivivus'. Henry had the present design painted on the previously blank Round Table in Winchester, with himself occupying Arthur's chair.

In the reign of Elizabeth the Tudor myth grew more potent. Cadwallader was alleged to have foretold her in person. Her astrologer John Dee discussed whether Arthur's Britons had colonised America ahead of the Spaniards. The essential notion was that the long-ago monarchy of Arthur had been the 'true' Britain. Saxon and Norman conquests, civil wars and usurpations, had obscured its glory, but now, with the Tudors, the glory was returning. Elizabeth's England was Arthurian Britain over again. Naturally the myth faded with time, and with scepticism about Geoffrey's version of the past, but not while Spenser was living. Even in the enlightened eighteenth century Thomas Gray, in his poem *The Bard*, could depict a medieval visionary dismissing the Plantagenets and hailing the 'genuine kings, Britannia's issue' coming after them.

———◆———

Since Spenser never came near to describing Arthur's monarchy and relating it directly to Tudor England, he had to weave the Tudor myth into his allegory by other methods. He could do it by introducing a retrospect of the distant British past, as leading up to an Arthurian golden age; he could do it by inventing a prophetic revelation rising to an apogee in Elizabeth's reign; or he could do both. He did both. For the quasi-history leading to Arthur, he made use of Geoffrey of Monmouth. For a prophetic outpouring further on, leading to Elizabeth, he kept Merlin in reserve.

The first of these two passages is in Book II of *The Faerie Queene*, Canto X. The knight in this book is Sir Guyon, who embodies the virtue of Temperance. He is journeying with the young Prince Arthur, who has no clear notion of who he is or what is in store for him. After conquering hostile pagans – 'Paynims' – they meet a lady called Alma, who lives in a castle built on a complicated geometric design, with a resident staff. She welcomes the visitors and conducts them to a turret where three 'sages' live. One of them can foresee the future, one is omniscient about the present, the third is a compendium of historical knowledge. The third sage is immensely old: he remembers Methuselah, whom he outlived. His room is full of books and parchments. Guyon and Arthur admire this unique library. Guyon picks out a book on Fairyland, Arthur chooses a history of Britain – which, of course, contains the substance of a large part of Geoffrey's work. Spenser paraphrases Geoffrey, and adds some improvements. So far as *The Faerie Queene* has a chronology, Prince Arthur's perusal of the book is supposed to be happening in the reign of his father Uther, when Britons are still in the ascendant over the Saxons. It begins by recognising, like the Welsh text about 'Myrddin's Precinct', a time when this island had no human population at all.

> The land, which warlike Britons now possess,
> And therein have their mighty empire raised,
> In antique times was savage wilderness,
> Unpeopled, unmanured, unproved, unpraised.
>
> *(Canto X. Stanza v)*

Presently seafarers discovered it and began to settle, naming it Albion after its white cliffs (a frequent but questionable derivation, which Spenser follows). However, it was not totally lifeless. Spenser adopts Geoffrey's giants, and makes them more repulsive, with sub-human companions.

> But far inland a savage nation dwelt,
> Of hideous giants, and half-beastly men. (*X.vii*)

The poet will not commit himself as to where the giants came from. He hurries on to the arrival of Brutus and his Trojans, compressing it and dropping Geoffrey's elaborate preliminaries. They took possession of Albion, giving it its new name, and disposed of the giants. Spenser follows Geoffrey's account of several of Brutus's successors. He lingers over a few whom he finds interesting, such as the erudite Bladud who founded Bath Spa, and his fatal flying accident.

> Ensample of his wondrous faculty,
> Behold the boiling baths at Cairbadon,
> Which seethe with secret fire eternally,
> And in their entrails, full of quick brimstone,
> Nourish the flames, which they are warmed upon,
> That to their people wealth they forth do well,
> And health to every foreign nation:
> Yet he at last contending to excel
> The reach of men, through flight into fond mischief fell.
>
> (X.xxvi)

Spenser paraphrases the story of Leir and his three daughters. This passage, rather than the original, may have been Shakespeare's source for *King Lear*.

Britain's royal line comes to an end after seven hundred years. Spenser skims over the next dynasty and the Roman period. Then he tells the tale of Vortigern letting the Saxons in, and the sons of King Constantine, Aurelius Ambrosius and Uther, returning from exile to depose him. The stanzas about these crucial events are typical of the rather perfunctory treatment given to much of Geoffrey's *History*. But Spenser is determined to follow him conscientiously, partly because of the way he intends to use the *History* later. And he does not follow him unthinkingly. He notices places where an important person has been left out, and fills the gap. For instance, Geoffrey omits the British queen Boudicca and her heroic revolt against the Romans, so Spenser, calling her 'Bunduca', puts her in at considerable length, giving her twenty-two lines, more than most of the kings get. He also has a few words about Joseph of Arimathea and his bringing of the Holy Grail to Britain; Geoffrey does not mention this legend, and it was probably not current in his time.

When Vortigern is out of the way, a break ensues which might be hard to parallel in English poetry. Aurelius reigns till he is poisoned, and then. . .

> After him Uther, which Pendragon hight,
> Succeeding (X.*lxviii*)

The text ends without even a full stop, and this is how it is in the imaginary book which Arthur is studying. The reason is that in *Faerie Queene* time, Uther is now reigning, and the book doesn't reveal what is coming next. Arthur seems to know very little about his deceased predecessors and even his living father. He is mildly shocked by the sudden conclusion or rather non-conclusion. Still, he is inspired by what he has been reading.

> At last quite ravished with delight, to hear
> The royal offspring of his native land,
> Cried out, Dear country, O how dearly dear
> Ought thy remembrance, and perpetual band
> Be to thy foster child! (X.*lxix*)

He will eventually go on in due course, as *King* Arthur, to be a more than worthy successor of his British forerunners. This part of the Tudor myth is securely in place.

━┿━ ☳◈☷ ━┿━

No one in *The Faerie Queene* foretells Arthur's actual reign. It is going to be described in detail when Spenser's grand design is completed. But the future beyond it must be glimpsed, with the later fulfilment of Arthurian promise in the Tudors and in the glories of Elizabeth. Here Merlin is indispensable as Britain's arch-prophet. In Book III the reader meets him.

Spenser introduces him gradually, at first offstage, as 'the great Magician'. The second canto tells of a magical looking-glass he made for a British king, Ryence; or, to be more precise, a magical glass globe, which showed anything in the world to a person whom it concerned.

> It virtue had, to show in perfect sight,
> Whatever thing was in the world contained,
> Betwixt the lowest earth and heaven's height,
> So that it to the looker appertained. (*II.xix*)

Ryence kept the globe as an early-warning device, to show the approach of rebels or enemies. One day, however, his daughter Britomart happened to go into the room where he kept it. Allegorically, Britomart represents Chastity. Not total sexual denial. She has a destined partner, and in the course of an exciting life, she will resist all advances and assaults till their long-delayed and legitimate union. Spenser takes her name from mythology, in which Britomartis is a Cretan nymph who throws herself into the sea to escape the importunities of King

137

Minos. The nymph is a close companion of the ever-virginal Artemis.

When Britomart entered the room with the magic globe in it, she was wondering, in a purely speculative way, about a future husband. The globe promptly showed her a handsome knight, and she fell in love with him, without having a clue as to his identity. After a succession of depressed days and restless nights, Britomart's old nurse Glauce discussed the problem with her and tried counter-measures without success. In case this tale of frustrated passion may be getting tedious, Spenser explains that it is leading up to the 'goodly ancestry' of his glorious sovereign. The reader will naturally want to know how.

Glauce decided that the two of them should go to the magician who made the glass – namely, Merlin – and ask how the visionary knight could be found. Spenser's account of the inquiry is amazing. To begin with, Glauce knows where to look for Merlin, and he is in the right place mythologically.

> Forthwith themselves disguising, both in strange
> And base attire, that none might them bewray,
> To Maridunum, that is now by change
> Of name Cayr-Merdin called, they took their way. (*III.vii*)

Several stanzas present the dweller in this place as an unparalleled being, almost a god in fact, though Spenser as a devout Protestant cannot spell it out.

> Merlin had in magic more insight
> Than ever him before or after living wight.

> For he by words could call out of the sky
> Both Sun and Moon, and make them him obey:
> The land to sea, and sea to mainland dry,
> And darksome night he eke could turn to day. (*III.xi–xii*)

Glauce and Britomart have to go a little way up the River Tywi to find the spot where Merlin has been living in retirement since his Tintagel performance and the conception of Arthur. Spenser tells us what Geoffrey conspicuously doesn't – where Merlin was, and what he was doing, in the gap of time between that event and Arthur's succession. His abode is a subterranean retreat, the cave under Merlin's Hill that figures in the local lore of Carmarthen.

> There the wise Merlin whilom wont (they say)
> To make his wonne [dwelling] low underneath the ground,
> In a deep delve, far from the view of day,
> That of no living wight he might be found,
> When he so counselled with his sprites encompassed round.
>
> (*III.vii*)

A piece of guidebook advice follows. Spenser, however, is not well informed. He thinks the cave can still be visited, and his local geography is a muddle: the river is not the Barry, and Dynevore Castle is too far from Carmarthen. However . . .

> And if thou ever happen that same way
> To travel, go to see that dreadful place:
> It is a hideous hollow cave (they say)
> Under a rock that lies a little space
> From the swift Barry, tumbling down apace,

Amongst the woody hills of Dynevowr;
But dare thou not, I charge, in any case,
To enter into that same baleful bower,
For fear the cruel fiends should thee unwares devour.

(III.viii)

If you listen carefully, you can hear metallic noises – iron chains rattling, cauldrons rumbling. The reason is that when Merlin lived there, he had a whole team of spirits at his command, obedient to him but dangerous to anyone else. He put them to work building a wall of brass round Carmarthen. Then, during King Arthur's reign, he was fatally allured by the Damsel in the Lake, and emerged from his cave to go to her, ordering the spirits not to cease working in his absence. As we know, his inamorata caught him in a magical trap and he never returned. The spirits under his spell could not leave off their activity, although nothing was coming of it. The wall never got built, yet you can still hear the noises underground.

To revert to Spenser's narrative, Glauce and Britomart arrived at the cave-mouth and hesitated. Finally they dared to go in.

First entering, the dreadful Mage they found
Deep buried 'bout work of wondrous end,
And writing strange characters in the ground,
With which the stubborn fiends he to his service bound.

(III.xiv)

Merlin was not surprised to see the two women. He knew they were on their way. But he asked them to state their business as if he did not. Glauce tried to explain without actually mentioning the magic glass, or identifying the princess Britomart, but of course Merlin understood everything.

He replied prophetically. The glass was incidental. What mattered was Britomart's destiny and the greatness of her descendants. The knight in the vision, her future spouse, was Artegall, of the family of Arthur's mother. Artegall is not in Geoffrey of Monmouth, but Spenser gives several stanzas as the substance of Merlin's prophecy, adapted from a passage in the *History* about the British kings who follow Arthur. They are made out to be prophesied descendants of Artegall and Britomart.

One is Vortiporius. He actually did rule part of Wales in the sixth century. The name Latinises his British one, Voteporix. A memorial stone with this name on it, presumably his monument, was found in 1895 near Haverfordwest and is now in Carmarthen County Museum. His son Malgo, in Merlin's prophecy, is also real: he is Maelgwn, a famous King of Gwynedd in North Wales, associated with Anglesey and Deganwy, and remembered by contemporaries as tall, brave, generous but erratic. He died in the 540s, a victim of a plague that ravaged western Britain and shifted the balance of population in favour of the Anglo-Saxons.

After Maelgwn there was nothing left that could count as a kingdom of Britain, even for the most wishful thinker. So Spenser has Merlin go on to talk of various Welsh and Saxon kings and their troubled reigns; he mentions Cadwallader, the alleged ancestor of Henry VII. At last, he says, the long-hidden Tudors, the real Britons, living unobtrusively on the island of Mona (Anglesey), will come out into the open. They will restore the true British monarchy, culminating in the almost Messianic Elizabeth.

Tho when the term is full accomplishid,
Then shall a spark of fire, which hath long-while
Been in the ashes raked up and hid,
Be freshly kindled in the fruitful Isle
Of Mona, where it lurked in exile;
Which shall break forth into bright burning flame,
And reach into the house, that bears the style
Of royal majesty and sovereign name,
So shall the Briton blood the crown again reclaim.

Thenceforth eternal union shall be made
Between the nations different afore,
And sacred Peace shall lovingly persuade
The warlike minds, to learn her goodly lore,
And civil arms to exercise no more;
Then shall a royal virgin reign, which shall
Stretch her white rod over the Belgic shore,
And the great Castle smite so sore withal
That it shall make him shake, and shortly learn to fall.

(III.xlviii)

The 'great Castle' is imperial Spain, symbolised by the arms of Castile.

'But yet the end is not.' Well, no. Merlin evidently sees what will come next, but Spenser, unable to look beyond the victory over the Armada, does not. He has to check the flow, and remembers the prophet's 'controlling spirit'.

. . . There Merlin stayed
As overcomen of the spirit's power
Or other ghastly spectacle dismayed,
That secretly he saw, yet not discoure [discover, reveal];

Which sudden fit, and half ecstatic stour
When the two fearful women saw, they grew
Greatly confused in behaviour;
At last the fury passed, to former hue
He turned again, and cheerful looks (as erst) did shew.

(III.l)

After a further elucidation the visitors take their leave, and
Britomart sets out on the adventures the poet has in store for
her.

Merlin does not appear again. However, an ambiguity
overhangs him. Was Britomart's vision entirely accidental? Or
did Merlin arrange everything, making the magic glass for this
express purpose, having it placed where she would see it, and
thus bringing together the couple who are needed for the
perpetuation of British royalty? Imaginative fiction should not
be probed too hard, as if it were reality. Still, there would be a
certain logical fitness in Merlin's masterminding the whole
business. He contrived the advent of Arthur at Tintagel. Perhaps
he is also contriving the succession that will lead to the advent
of Elizabeth, as a long-term national investment.

Mainly because of the propagandist content, this episode raises
curious issues. It involves Spenser in questionable transitions
from one kind of story to another. Prince Arthur, for instance,
adventuring in the allegorical Fairyland, is quite incompatible
with the secret heir of legend, yet he is being visibly groomed
for the same British kingship.

Britomart and Glauce have to step out of allegory altogether,
on to the real map and into real time. Merlin himself is not an

allegory, he is historical, or reputedly historical. During Uther's reign (a passage further on pinpoints the date) he lives in his underground chamber, which Spenser says is still extant in his own day and can be visited, however confused he may be by Welsh geography. He is clear about the connection with Carmarthen, a real place, and about the proprietary aspect: Merlin plans to surround it with a wall.

To recapitulate, Merlin is a wizard of immense power, able to cause cosmic disturbances. Around him are spirits whom he controls by magical formulae, so completely that when he goes away they continue following his orders like robots. Spenser calls him a Mage, and he is a super-Mage such as Renaissance fantasy dwelt upon, relocated in the fifth century. To some extent he anticipates Prospero in *The Tempest*. But the spirits he commands are dangerous creatures. Spenser calls them fiends. He never tells us where Merlin came from, or how he achieved mastery over his alarming team.

What actually happens in the consultation? Merlin's cave is not oracular; Glauce does not come to it like a Greek coming to Delphi. She has a specific personal inquiry, arising out of the magic globe. He is prepared for it, and responds with his long prophecy about Britomart's descendants down to Elizabeth Tudor. It is not clear how he does this. From Robert de Boron onwards Merlin is assumed to have knowledge of the future, and he proves it to the kings he has dealings with. But this knowledge was given him at birth, or rather in embryo, by the devil who fathered him and could not take it back. Spenser, as a devout Christian, never mentions the paternity, or, for that matter, Geoffrey's earlier story of the incubus demon. Whatever his private opinion of these popish fables, he removes the basis of the prophecy. Also, gratuitously, he surrounds Merlin with a sinister entourage that would hardly inspire confidence. Simply as a poetic device, could he have employed a devil – even a devil in the unmentioned background – to enable Merlin to prophesy Queen Elizabeth?

His only recourse is to recall Merlin's 'controlling spirit' in Geoffrey of Monmouth, who may be a god but at least keeps devils out of the way, and introduce this being to finish the prophecy, with an implication that he was there all along and Merlin summoned him at the beginning; as he did at his confrontation with Vortigern when the same being inspired the original prophecies.

Outside England the Tudor myth had no real equivalent. France, however, harboured something like it, though it was less potent and lacked the stimulus of apparent fulfilment. It had its own prophetic accompaniment, and even its own connection with Ariosto.

In the Middle Ages the tradition of Charlemagne, who had unified western Europe in a restored Empire and defeated Christendom's enemies, had generated the hope of a *Second* Charlemagne. He would bring a golden age, would establish universal peace, would – perhaps – be the principal agent in a transformation of Christianity. Some of these hopes were too extravagant to last. But the idea of a Second Charlemagne raising the French monarchy to unprecedented heights, with benefits all round, could still appeal; and Ariosto's popular epic, reactivating the Charlemagne legend for numerous readers, was a reminder. There was even some prophesying, and a figure emerged who became, after a fashion, a French retort to Merlin.

One of those who talked about the national hope was Nostradamus. 'Nostradamus' is a Latinisation of the name of Michel de Nostredame. He was born in 1503 to a Provençal Jewish family who converted to Catholicism. He practised as a doctor unobtrusively and successfully, and then wandered for six years, mainly in Italy, conferring with assorted scholars, astrologers and alchemists. Finally he settled at Salon in Provence with a wife (his second), who bore several children.

He began publishing astrological almanacs with predictions for each year. These were unimpressive. In 1555, however, he launched the much greater project that immortalised him. He started putting together long-term predictions in rhymed quatrains, and grouped the quatrains in sets of a hundred called Centuries (the word has nothing to do with periods of time). They were not arranged in any logical order, and he may have deliberately jumbled them. Centuries appeared at intervals for the rest of his life, and posthumously.

Nostradamus made his reputation primarily on the basis of a single widely publicised forecast. The same is true of one or two public prognosticators in modern times, such as the newspaper astrologer R.H. Naylor and the Washington psychic Jeane Dixon, but Nostradamus was more effective in keeping prophecies going. He succeeded initially with a tragic accident. People at the French court, including the queen, Catherine de Medici, were already taking notice of him. In July 1559 her husband King Henri II rode in a tournament against a younger opponent, the Comte de Montgomery. When they clashed, Montgomery lowered his lance a moment too late. The wooden tip splintered, penetrating Henri's insecure visor and entering his head beside an eye. The king was lowered from his horse, bleeding profusely, and died in agony ten days later.

Nostradamus had already published a quatrain that was seen as foreshadowing the tragedy. A translation runs as follows:

> The young lion will overcome the old one
> On the field of battle, in single combat;
> He will put out his eyes in a cage of gold,
> Two wounds one, then to die a cruel death.

This was not really so very brilliant, but 'two wounds one', a curious phrase, was apt. The blade of Montgomery's splintered lance did inflict a double wound: the larger splinter destroyed the king's eye, the smaller one pierced his throat. The fulfilment, at any rate, was close enough and shocking enough to convince the horrified French court.

From then on Nostradamus's cryptic quatrains, 942 in the final count, were widely read and discussed. As he hinted in a few of them, he recognised, and accepted, the hope of a Second Charlemagne, though not as emphatically as some enthusiasts. He did not anticipate anything apocalyptic. The Second Charlemagne would be simply a superlatively excellent French king. He would unite the nation and heal its wounds, but things would probably go on afterwards, the world would not come to an end with him.

His first tentative candidate was Henri II himself. If he did foresee the disaster at the tournament, he did not foresee that Henri would be the victim. For a while after that, he ceased to speculate. However, in 1564 a royal party visited Salon. With the adults was an 11-year-old prince, also named Henri. Nostradamus picked him out and made what appeared a most unlikely prediction: he would be King of Navarre, and presently of all France.

According to Chavigny, a biographer, Nostradamus was the first to suspect that *this* was the Henri who would fulfil the hope. In one of his later prophecies he said 'Vendôme' would oust the House of Lorraine. The prince had the title Duke of Vendôme.

He was justified by events. The boy became celebrated as Henri of Navarre, and in 1589 succeeded to the throne of France as Henri IV. It took him several years to achieve undisputed power, but Messianic notions began to cling to him. A pamphlet published in 1592 spelt it out: he was *Carolus Magnus Redivivus*, Charlemagne revived. The scientist and philosopher Giordano Bruno concurred. Henri took bold measures for national prosperity; he was one of the very few French kings to be regarded in retrospect as good. He ended the long miseries of France's Wars of Religion, extended toleration to the Protestants by the Edict of Nantes in 1598, and even invented a plan for universal peace, called the Grand Design. His assassination in 1610 left his main achievement intact.

The mystique lasted for a long time. Napoleon tried to exploit it by putting imperial insignia on his coach, crowning himself emperor, and carrying what was alleged to be Charlemagne's sceptre at the ceremony. In a letter to a cardinal asserting his right to dominate the Church, he wrote: 'I am Charlemagne.'

Nostradamus's lasting fame, however, was not based on speculations like these, but on his Centuries. It is said that they have been in print ever since. Certainly he has inspired endless attempts at interpretation. Few authors can have been harmed so much by their admirers. They have produced books and films crediting him with foretelling the rise of Hitler, aerial warfare, the Kennedy assassinations and much else in comparatively modern times. The trouble is that so many of his quatrains do look specific. They identify nations and prominent individuals, or at least hint at them; they occasionally name names; they refer to recognisable places, and to things that *could* happen there. Sometimes, if enough historical knowledge is brought to bear, they may seem to make sense, but it seldom is.

The waste of effort by amateurish commentators has been a pity, because their fancies have discredited Nostradamus more than he deserves. He does make some predictions that are genuinely interesting – not many, but some, and not in a random scatter, but interrelated and concentrated in a few quatrains. However they should be explained, they at least show to advantage beside the prognostications of self-appointed seers, psychics and unravellers of the Apocalypse generally.*

Most of this is not relevant to Merlin, but one point is, extremely so. At the beginning of the Centuries Nostradamus tells what he does. There is not a word about astrology, and even on the most favourable view, astrology could not account for the sort of detail that he includes in his prophecies. What he describes is a preparatory ritual based on the teachings of a late-Roman Neo-Platonist, Iamblichus. The practitioner – Nostradamus himself – sits alone at night in his study, wearing a robe and holding a wand. In front of him is a brass tripod like the tripod at Delphi that was used by Apollo's priestesses. On this is a bowl of water, into which he looks – a kind of 'scrying' or crystal-gazing. Becoming aware of a 'slight flame', probably a metaphor for the first gleam of inspiration, he lays the wand under the tripod and sprinkles a little water on his robe and his feet. A voice seems to speak to him, and he is momentarily afraid, but in the last line:

* See Ashe, *The Book of Prophecy* (London: Orion, 2002), chs 8 and 9.

Splendeur divine. Le divin pres s'assied.
Divine splendour. The god sits nearby.

Everything up to this point is simply a kind of self-hypnosis, but the final words are definite. Nostradamus prophesies by surrendering himself to a divine being (he repeats the crucial word) from whom the communications come. And likewise, of course, Merlin's controlling spirit takes possession of him. In France as in Britain, the prophet does not do it himself by a technique of his own. He invites the Other, and from the Other, god or spirit or whatever, the illumination proceeds, even if the recipient garbles it hopelessly or makes it incomprehensible. What actually happens may be a question for psychologists, but something does.

9

Shakespeare and Others

After Malory, English Arthurian romance went into virtual hibernation. Any echoes or sequels would have been merely imitative and anticlimactic. During the sixteenth century the Tudor myth flourished, and Spenser's enlistment of Merlin on its behalf gave it an interesting new role for readers of poetry, but the role was an offbeat one in an allegorical context, and it could never be a canonical element in the Matter of Britain.

Merlin had a scattered folklore fame. The mound at Marlborough had long been pointed out as his tumulus, though the notion, besides being based on a misunderstanding of the town's name, was inconsistent with the belief in his survival. Some at least of the local legends around Carmarthen – the legends of his hill, his grove, his cave, his stone, his tree – were already current. A few Cornish prophecies are on record. By the porch of St Levan's church, near Land's End, is an ancient cross, and beside this is a cleft rock, St Levan's stone. After Arthur fought a battle against the Danes at Vellandruchar, he was travelling with Merlin when they noticed the cleft rock. Merlin extemporised:

> When, with panniers astride,
> A pack-horse can ride
> Through St Levan's stone,
> The world will be done.

The gap is far too narrow. Merlin seems to be saying that in some way at present unforeseeable, the thing will happen; and this impossible event will be a portent of the end of the world. An objection, of course, is that Merlin would not have spoken English. He is also said to have made this couplet:

> When the Rame Head and Dodman meet,
> Man and woman will have cause to greet.

'Greet' means to weep. The two headlands are 40 miles apart. It would take a tremendous cataclysm to bring them together, and the upheaval would doubtless be a reason for woe.

More interesting is a prophecy about the fishing village of Mousehole. An offshore ledge appears on maps as Merlyn Rock. However, the name (Merlin Carreg) originally meant a rock at the south end of the quay. Merlin prophesied:

> There shall land on the Rock of Merlin
> Those who shall burn Paul, Penzance and Newlyn.

Just beyond the rock is Point Spaniard. This prophecy was fulfilled in July 1595 by a Spanish raid.

Four galleys, with attendant small craft, anchored in Mount's Bay. Two hundred men disembarked and set fire to Mousehole. There was one local casualty, Jenken Keigwin. His house survived and became an inn, the Keigwin Arms. Detachments went on to Paul and Newlyn and did further damage. The Spaniards then returned to their galleys and rowed to Penzance. Here four hundred men landed and started more fires. They celebrated Mass on a nearby hill (this was the one transitory success of the Catholic restoration intended by the Armada) and sailed away.

Richard Carew, who tells the story, says that when the local people were reproached for not putting up a fight, they quoted Merlin's prophecy to show that the attack was fated. The prophecy is on record soon after the raid, but cannot be proved to have been current before it; this may be a case of prophecy-after-the-event, like the first series of Merlin's in Geoffrey of Monmouth. Again, Merlin would not have spoken English. However, the locals quoted a Cornish version, and this is slightly more plausible:

> Ewra teyre a war meane Merlyn,
> Ara lesky Pawle, Pensanze ha Newlyn.

The famous English raid on Cadiz in the following year was a reprisal for this one.

While the evidence for Merlin's popular reputation is sketchy, it was well enough established to be made fun of in *King Lear*. During the storm, when Kent is leading Lear and the Fool to shelter, the Fool pauses before following them, with a speech that seems oddly inappropriate in the circumstances.

> I'll speak a prophecy ere I go:
> When priests are more in word than matter;
> When brewers mar their malt with water;
> When nobles are their tailors' tutors;
> No heretics burn'd, but wenches' suitors;
> When every case in law is right,
> No squire in debt, nor no poor knight;
> When slanders do not live in tongues;
> Nor cutpurses come not to throngs;
> When usurers tell their gold i' the field;

And bawds and whores do churches build; –
Then shall the realm of Albion
Come to great confusion:
Then comes the time, who lives to see 't,
That going shall be us'd with feet.
This prophecy Merlin shall make; for I live before his time.

When I first read these lines, under a vague impression that King Lear and Merlin were both mythical and dateless, the Fool's parting shot seemed just a silly joke. But Geoffrey of Monmouth (Shakespeare's probable source for the story of King Lear) justifies it. The Fool is more than a thousand years earlier, and to make somebody else prophesy Merlin, not the other way around, is an acceptable bit of comedy.

Two lesser dramatists, Thomas Heywood and William Rowley, kept interest alive with fictitious 'prophecies of Merlin'. These were being quoted quite seriously as late as 1969. Merlin's mantle was still worth donning. The astrologer William Lilly (1602–81), in imitation perhaps of Nostradamus's early efforts, published an annual almanac of forecasts under the pseudonym 'Merlinus Anglicus Junior'. He was a professional in his field, making money not only by casting horoscopes but by teaching others to do it. In 1648 and again in 1651 he foretold disasters in London around 1665, including 'sundry fires and a consuming plague'. The Great Plague happened in 1665 and the Great Fire in 1666. Lilly was suspected of starting the fire himself, or at least of knowing arsonists. From 1680 on another astrologer, John Partridge, brought out an almanac of his own as 'Merlinus Liberatus', and kept it going until his annihilation by Jonathan Swift.

The strange thing is that Lilly and Partridge should have assumed Merlin's name at all, when he is never portrayed as an astrologer. Robert de Boron does introduce astrology, but as a sinister form of divination practised by Vortigern's magicians, who want Merlin killed. For Lilly and Partridge the name that they assumed simply implied foretelling the future, and astrology was supposed to be a method of doing this, whether the original Merlin practised it or not. Lilly claimed psychic powers of a sort, unrelated to astrology. He obtained permission to look for hidden treasure in the cloister of Westminster Abbey, and began to search with dowsing rods. However, a storm blew his candle out and he blamed unsympathetic onlookers for spoiling the experiment.

In spite of this irresponsible exploitation of the name, serious interest in Merlin had not expired. In 1613 Michael Drayton revealed a literary awareness in his long poetic survey of Britain, *Polyolbion*:

> Of Merlin and his skill what region doth not hear?
> The world shall still be full of Merlin everywhere.
> A thousand lingering years his prophecies have run,
> And scarcely shall have end till time itself be done.

Actual literary production, however, was confined for the moment to a play written about 1620, entitled *The Birth of Merlin*. It was not printed at once, and the Puritans' closure of the theatres consigned it to obscurity for a long time, but in 1662, after the Restoration, it was published at last with two names on the title-page. One was William Rowley, the other was William Shakespeare. The greater name was attached quite illegitimately in order to attract interest and assist sales.

Unfortunately, nothing in the text suggests that Shakespeare did have a hand in it. Rowley collaborated with several contemporary dramatists, but not with the foremost of them all.

The subtitle was *The Childe hath found his Father*, and Rowley's novel idea was that Merlin should be brought face to face with his diabolic parent. At the beginning he has not yet been born. His heavily pregnant mother Joan is uncertain how her child was begotten, and she is trying to find out before the actual birth. Joan and her brother, the Clown, are comic most of the time. But the play has a lively mix of dramatic action, with reminiscences of Geoffrey of Monmouth, several sub-plots and magical effects that occasionally recall *The Tempest*.

In the first act King Aurelius has defeated the Saxons, and they are sending an emissary to discuss a peace treaty. The emissary turns out to be an alluring woman, Artesia. Aurelius tries to dictate terms, but becomes confused, until at last he negotiates a deal favourable to the Saxons. The Britons around him are horrified.

Joan and her loyal but ludicrous brother are seen trudging through a wood. They remain the principal characters, and their dialogue helps to hold the play together. Joan remembers being accosted in this wood by a well-dressed and courteous gentleman. He enters and turns out to be Uther (spelt Uter), who has been missing for some time. Is he the father of the imminent child? Uter evades the question. He loves another woman, and has been composing complimentary verses addressed to her.

Aurelius marries Artesia. The wedding is attended by a Saxon magician, Proximus. Hostility to the royal match is running high; Edol, the Earl of Chester, rides away to lead British resistance. Proximus entertains the guests by conjuring up apparitions of Achilles and Hector, but a patriotic Hermit, who also has power over spirits, banishes them and spoils the effect. It turns out that the woman to whom Uter is addressing poems is Artesia herself, his brother's new bride.

Joan and the Clown are still searching. They arrive at court and the Clown makes inquiries without success. The Devil who is actually the child's father appears to Joan; she can see and hear him, but her brother can only hear. She follows the Devil into the wood. The child is born, with supernatural manifestations.

Merlin grows up even faster than he does in romance. He looks 'like an artichoke' and enters reading a book, and proclaiming that he intends to 'sound the depth of Arts, Learning, Wisdom, Knowledge'. The Clown realises who the father is. Several of the characters converge on Vortigern's castle. Artesia, who has been treacherous all along, is plotting to kill both Aurelius and Uter. The duped Aurelius is persisting in his attempted Saxon alliance. Vortigern's tower collapses, as usual, and the human sacrifice is planned. But Merlin outwits Proximus, the Saxon magician. After an altercation with his evil progenitor, he closes him in a rock. He also promises to raise an enduring monument for his mother, and this turns out to be Stonehenge.

Artesia has succeeded in killing Aurelius, but she is imprisoned. She has a truly Jacobean exit line: 'Thy brother's poisoned, but I wanted more.' Uter becomes king, and Merlin shows the court a magical pageant of the future glories of Uter's son Arthur.

Rowley could still take it for granted that the audience, or a sufficiently large proportion of it, would understand what his play was about. But the Arthurian tide was ebbing. The Tudor myth could not be sustained long in the absence of Tudors, and under James I the mystique was less patriotic and more political. It was becoming entangled with James's notions about his Divine Right, and his conflict with Parliament. Royalists could still cite Geoffrey's *History* as evidence that Britain was, and had always been, monarchical. However, supporters of Parliament were casting the first real doubt on Geoffrey's historicity. They were also discovering Anglo-Saxon institutions and laws, and finding better precedents.

A literary consequence of the great dispute – which, under James's successor Charles I, led to the Civil War – was that an English Arthur epic which might have been written never actually was. Milton considered the idea but dropped it for several reasons. One was that he shared the growing scepticism about Arthur's existence. Another, probably, was that as a strong supporter of Parliament he could not see his way to writing an epic about a king and his court. At that time it would have had to follow in the track of Ariosto and Spenser, and Milton, as he put it himself, was not inclined to 'dissect / With long and tedious havoc fabl'd knights / In Battels feign'd'.

Having settled on his preferred biblical theme, he broke completely with Ariosto and Spenser even in his poetic form. He planned first to present the Fall of Man as a play. Then, when he undertook *Paradise Lost* as a full-scale epic, he rejected both Ariosto's *ottava rima* and Spenser's nine-line stanza, and wrote it in blank verse, hitherto little used outside drama. When it was published, some of his readers were 'stumbled' by the absence of rhyme. He added a prefatory note in quite a combative tone, describing rhyme as 'no necessary Adjunct or true Ornament of Poem or good Verse . . . but the Invention of a barbarous Age, to set off wretched matter and lame Meeter'.

Milton, as a Puritan, could not have made anything of Merlin. He wrote a masque for performance at Ludlow Castle, in which a magician, Comus, is a wholly sinister figure, the son of Bacchus and the Homeric sorceress Circe who turned men into pigs. Comus bewitches a lady and tries to draw her into the obscene revelry in his palace. Her resolute chastity protects her, and her brothers rescue her. As for prophecy, the last two books of *Paradise Lost* are full of it, but it is all prophecy of scriptural matters, in a future revealed to Adam by the archangel Michael.

So the Arthur epic was considered and rejected by Milton. It was also considered and rejected by John Dryden, the chief poet of the Restoration. His motive for rejecting it was probably because he could make more money by writing plays. However, he did eventually produce the libretto of an opera called *King Arthur, or The British Worthy* (1691), with music by Purcell. His operatic king fights Saxons, loves a princess named Emmeline, and looks forward to British-Saxon amity. The only magic in the opera is hostile. Again there is nobody with a role comparable to Merlin's.

The project for an Arthur epic, which two major poets had declined to take up, was unfortunately seized upon by a third poet whose handling of it was disastrous. Sir Richard Blackmore, a fashionable doctor who scribbled epics in his coach between house calls, perpetrated not one but two on Arthur. He borrowed freely from both Milton and Dryden, and gave his epics an inexcusable political bias by making Arthur's career an allegory of William III's. It paid, but it associated Arthur with poor and pretentious writing, and he faded from English literature for a while, as a 'Gothic' spectre with whom the rational good sense of an enlightened era could not concern itself. Very little is on record in the eighteenth century except for a few plays for private audiences who liked expensive effects in the 'masque' tradition. It is interesting that most of the surviving titles have 'Merlin' in them – for instance, *Merlin's Hermitage*; *Merlin in Love*; *Merlin, or the Devil of Stonehenge* – and none has 'Arthur'.

Merlin resurfaced in three settings. One was Sir Walter Scott's verse tale *The Bride of Triermain*. The magician makes a brief appearance to stop a tourney in which a knight has been killed, and to condemn the woman whose charms have caused the fighting to a long slumber in Sleeping Beauty style. Scott had a word of praise for Anne Bannerman, who wrote in the fashionable Gothic mode. Her poems include *The Prophecy of Merlin*, a ballad in forty-three dramatic stanzas about the passing and return of Arthur.

The other relevant production is an eccentric poem by a most unexpected person, William Wordsworth. Called *The Egyptian Maid*, it was published in 1835. At the beginning, in Cornwall, a mysterious air-borne vessel is hovering in the sky:

> While Merlin paced the Cornish sands,
> Forth-looking toward the rocks of Scilly,
> The pleased Enchanter was aware
> Of a bright Ship that seemed to hang in air,
> Yet was the work of mortal hands,
> And took from men her name – THE WATER LILY.

(It is hard to avoid the suspicion that Merlin is looking at the rocks of Scilly because Wordsworth needed a rhyme for 'lily'.) Merlin admires the flying ship, but, through some perverseness of will, he takes a dislike to it, raises a storm and forces it down. An Egyptian princess, insensible and seemingly dead, is cast ashore on a rock. Nina, the Lady of the Lake, takes charge of the princess and orders Merlin to convey her to Arthur's court at Caerleon. He does so, in a swan-drawn chariot. The court gathers round. It emerges that one of the older knights is the princess's father. Though she lived in Egypt as a heathen, he had plans for her marriage. Now he mourns her apparent death. Merlin, however, tells him that if the knights approach one by one and touch her hand, the one whose touch restores her to life is her destined husband.

Several try – Agravain, Kay, Percival, Gawain, Lancelot – but she remains motionless. At last Galahad touches her and she recovers. They are married. This is a glaring departure from Galahad's usual virginity. Only the contact with his saintliness could free her from the Egyptian spell.

The Egyptian Maid was not a considerable poem, but its author would soon be Poet Laureate. The tide of interest was just starting to turn. Wordsworth's successor in the Laureateship would bring a new beginning.

10

Magic, Monarchy and Morals

Alfred, Lord Tennyson, was the first English author after Malory to attempt a whole Arthurian cycle, but his *Idylls of the King* do not form a continuous narrative. They are Arthurian episodes written at intervals over a long period from 1855 on, and arranged in a fairly logical order. Tennyson was a rare phenomenon, a major poet whose poetry was genuinely popular, a best-seller.

If you had asked a middle-class Victorian what poetry was, the answer might well have been 'the sort of thing that Tennyson writes'. He wrote a substantial amount of it, and it brought in a substantial income.

Tennyson was born in the family of a comfortably off clergyman at Somersby in Lincolnshire. As a Cambridge undergraduate, with no definite academic or professional aims, he was friendly with a group of gifted and idealistic students. One was Arthur Henry Hallam, the son of a well-known historian. Alfred's attachment to this particular friend amounted almost to adoration. It was not a homosexual relationship, at least in any overt sense, and Alfred was to make a happy and successful marriage. But when Arthur Hallam died suddenly while abroad, Alfred was plunged into an abyss of grief where he remained for years.

Losing any conventional faith in immortality, he longed to believe that Hallam was not gone for ever and they would meet again. This obsession certainly played a part in turning his thoughts toward Arthur Hallam's royal namesake, the legendary king who was immortal and would return. In one of his poems the two are indistinguishable.

His misery was all the deeper because of the current undermining of Christian faith. There had never been much sympathy in England for the continental Enlightenment, which was associated with the old enemy France and the horrors of the French Revolution. However, even in that pre-Darwin time, a threat was gathering from science, especially geology. Hitherto it had been possible, if with an effort, to believe that the world was created in 4004 BC, the biblical date; that the whole human race was descended from eight individuals in the Ark, who alone survived the Flood; and that all animals – land animals, anyhow – were descended from the couples that Noah took aboard with him. But it was growing clear that Earth was much older than the Bible said, that a single recent ancestry of the whole human race was incredible, and that many species had existed that did not fit into the scriptural scheme. Tennyson aired his doubts, at first anonymously, in a long series of poems under the title *In Memoriam*. He arrived at last at a faith that was proof against geology, and accommodated a trust that Arthur Hallam still lived, if in a way that was beyond our comprehension.

Tennyson began his Arthurian series, characteristically perhaps, at the gloomy end, with the king wounded and dying after his last battle. The poem *Morte d'Arthur* is presented as an epic fragment read aloud at a party. This fiction allowed Tennyson to add an epilogue, a dream-sequence about Arthur returning in a ship 'like a modern gentleman of stateliest port' amid shouts of 'Arthur is come again: he cannot die'. The phrase 'modern gentleman' alluded to Victoria's husband Prince Albert. Tennyson was appointed Poet Laureate in 1850, and took the honour more seriously than most. He was intensely loyal to the sovereign, and admired her Consort – at the time this was a minority view. Albert's early and tragic death, like Hallam's, reanimated the Arthurian theme for him.

Victoria's daughter Princess Alice expressed a wish that Tennyson should 'idealise' her late father in verse. He felt unable to do so, but approached the assignment symbolically. To an edition of some of the *Idylls* already written, he prefixed a dedication:

> These to His Memory – since he held them dear,
> Perchance as finding there unconsciously
> Some image of himself – I dedicate,
> I dedicate, I consecrate with tears –
> These Idylls.
>
> (*Dedication*, 1–5)

He praised Albert for 'wearing the white flower of a blameless life', and the infelicitous adjective 'blameless' became annexed in his verse to King Arthur, who, indeed, came to resemble Albert even in his appearance: he had a moustache, not a common detail in poetry.

In an epilogue addressed to the Queen when the cycle was at last finished or nearly so, he recalled her husband, and expressed his attitude to the legend in language calculated to reassure her.

For one to whom I made it o'er his grave
Sacred, accept this old imperfect tale,
New-old, and shadowing Sense at war with Soul,
Ideal manhood closed in real man,
Rather than that gray king, whose name, a ghost,
Streams like a cloud, man-shaped, from mountain peak,
And cleaves to cairn and cromlech still; or him
Of Geoffrey's book, or him of Malleor's, one
Touch'd by the adulterous finger of a time
That hover'd between war and wantonness.

(To the Queen, 35–44)

The legend, in Tennyson's hands, was allegorical or at least symbolic and therefore respectable. Elsewhere he said: 'By Arthur I always meant the soul, and by the Round Table the passions and capacities of a man.'

What it amounted to was that while he kept much of Malory, even paraphrasing him closely at times, he imposed Victorian moral values, not always successfully. Some of the *Idylls* are magnificent, or, at least, have magnificent passages. Some have been condemned by critics as 'verse-novelettes'. But one way or another, Tennyson was always trying to expound an ideal of spiritually inspired monarchy. He met Victoria at Osborne in 1862. Henceforth the relation of Laureate to Queen, which he expressed in the epilogue just quoted, was romantic and chivalrous.

The opening *Idyll*, *The Coming of Arthur*, was not the first to be written. Tennyson added it when it became evident that the series would need an introduction and an overall framework.

It begins with post-Roman Britain ravaged by the heathen. Aurelius and Uther have fought and died; warring petty kings are rending the land apart; wilderness is encroaching, wild beasts are multiplying – it is an image of spiritual disintegration. Arthur appears, assembles a chosen band of followers and turns the tide. Merlin has been taking care of the child who is now grown up. Merlin's 'hour has come' and he proclaims Arthur as Uther's heir. In spite of vociferous protests, he has him crowned. The protests continue.

Merlin in the *Idylls* is definitely a magician, and does great public works for the king – Tennyson's glancing reminiscence, perhaps, of the Stonehenge story. But there is no attempt to explain who he is or where he came from, or why he ever had charge of the child; and no one seems to know, except, presumably, Arthur. Also, no one seems to be sure who Arthur is himself, except, presumably, Merlin. Here at the outset Tennyson plants a doubt that will be functional about the credentials of authority, doubt that will be a factor in the monarchy's eventual failure. Is Arthur Uther's son? If so, is he legitimate? Most of the discussion about him is hearsay, attributed to the Queen of Orkney, whom Tennyson, for some reason, calls Bellicent.

She is talking to Guinevere's father Leodogran, who is naturally uncertain about allowing his daughter's marriage to such an ambiguous suitor. Bellicent has seen Arthur's court where the Round Table is established, and is impressed. The description assumes that a good deal of the 'official' story has already happened. Tennyson is not going to retell it.

> When he spake and cheer'd his Table Round
> With large, divine, and comfortable words,

Beyond my tongue to tell thee – I beheld
From eye to eye thro' all their Order flash
A momentary likeness of the King . . .
And there I saw mage Merlin, whose vast wit
And hundred winters are but as the hands
Of loyal vassals toiling for their liege.
And near him stood the Lady of the Lake,
Who knows a subtler magic than his own . . .
There likewise I beheld Excalibur
Before him [Arthur] at his crowning borne, the sword
That rose from out the bosom of the lake. . . .
The blade so bright
That men are blinded by it – on one side,
Graven in the oldest tongue of all the world,
'Take me', but turn the blade and ye shall see,
And written in the speech ye speak yourself,
'Cast me away'. And sad was Arthur's face
Taking it, but old Merlin counsell'd him,
'Take thou and strike! The time to cast away
Is yet far-off.'

(The Coming of Arthur, 266–307)

Leodogran still wants to know the circumstances of Uther's death and Arthur's arrival. Tennyson has a difficulty here, because he must keep Tintagel, yet eliminate Uther's scandalous exploit. The result is a mixture of vivid poetry and final evasion. Bellicent quotes a conversation with Bleys, Merlin's reputed master, who recently died. He told her of the dark night when Uther passed away at Tintagel, lamenting that he had no heir. Bleys and Merlin were present. Directly after his death, they went outside to breathe.

Then from the castle gateway by the chasm
Descending thro' the dismal night — a night
In which the bounds of heaven and earth were lost —
Beheld, so high upon the dreary deeps
It seem'd in heaven, a ship, the shape thereof
A dragon wing'd, and all from stem to stern
Bright with a shining people on the decks,
And gone as soon as seen. And then the two
Dropt to the cove, and watch'd the great sea fall,
Wave after wave, each mightier than the last,
Till last, a ninth one, gathering half the deep
And full of voices, slowly rose and plunged
Roaring, and all the wave was in a flame:
And down the wave and in the flame was borne
A naked babe, and rode to Merlin's feet,
Who stoopt and caught the babe, and cried 'The King!
Here is an heir for Uther!' And the fringe
Of that great breaker, sweeping up the strand,
Lash'd at the wizard as he spake the word,
And all at once all round him rose in fire,
So that the child and he were clothed in fire.
And presently thereafter follow'd calm,
Free sky and stars.

(The Coming of Arthur, 369–91)

The child, Bleys assured Bellicent before he died himself, was
'he who reigns' – Arthur, now adult. She hardly knew what to
make of this. Even if it was all true, what was the dragon-ship
and who were the shining people? She managed to find Merlin
himself, and asked him point-blank, but only got a riddling
answer:

Rain, rain, and sun; a rainbow in the sky!
A young man will be wiser by and by;
An old man's wit may wander ere he die.
Rain, rain, and sun! A rainbow on the lea!
And truth is this to me, and that to thee;
And truth or clothed or naked let it be.
Rain, sun, and rain! And the free blossom blows;
Sun, rain, and sun! and where is he who knows?
From the great deep to the great deep he goes.
                              (*The Coming of Arthur*, 402–10)

The last line was manifestly the critical one, but she was not told what it meant. Tennyson repeats it at the end of the whole series, when Arthur is vanishing in the distance; it is still not explained. Bellicent also heard Merlin say that Arthur would be wounded but would not die. He would return. Once again, part of the story is already taken for granted.

Bellicent tells Leodogran that whatever the truth about Arthur, he will certainly achieve great things, and there is no reason Guinevere should not marry him. The wedding proceeds, with lavish ceremony and a choral accompaniment by the knights. But the straight question 'What are Arthur's credentials?' remains unanswered; and for readers who know what is to come (and Tennyson assumes that most of his readers do know) the wedding scene is ironic.

He seems to have entered a realm of pure imagination, yet this is not so. The antecedents are not easily shaken off. Surprisingly, he goes out of his way to remind us that we are still, in Geoffrey of Monmouth's time-frame. The wedding feast is interrupted by 'Lords from Rome, / The slowly fading mistress of the world', who demand tribute as in Geoffrey's *History*. Arthur refuses, with a memorable line:

> The old order changeth, yielding place to new.
> (*The Coming of Arthur*, 508)

No military response follows. The lords go away annoyed, and the issue is unresolved. Arthur 'strove with Rome', but throughout the *Idylls* we are never told how.

This is not the only place where Tennyson, despite his protestations to Victoria, touched on reality or quasi-reality. He not only studied Malory, he also investigated traditions which Malory knew nothing of, and travelled in the West Country familiarising himself with 'Arthurian' locations. Tintagel, of course, was one of them. Some of his information came from the eccentric Robert Hawker, vicar of Morwenstow and a poet in his own right, noted for sitting on an offshore rock wearing only seaweed.

In the *Idylls*, even when Tennyson does appear to have parted with reality, this is not always so. When Sir Gareth and two companions approach Camelot, Arthur's headquarters, it sounds like a visionary city that could never have existed.

> So, when their feet were planted on the plain
> That broaden'd toward the base of Camelot,
> Far off they saw the silver-misty morn
> Rolling her smoke about the Royal mount,
> That rose between the forest and the field.
> At times the summit of the high city flash'd;
> At times the spires and turrets half-way down
> Prick'd thro' the mist, at times the great gate shone
> Only, that open'd on the field below:
> Anon, the whole fair city had disappear'd.
> (*Gareth and Lynette*, 184–93)

In fact, the topography suggests that Tennyson did at least glance at the Cadbury hill-fort in Somerset, the only reputed 'Camelot' with any serious claim to a traditional basis. Cadbury is not the Camelot of romance, but excavation has shown that it was refortified in the second half of the fifth century by a British king with exceptional resources. Its association with the legend is now known to be medieval, not merely a literary fiction of the Renaissance.* If Tennyson made a detour to look at it, he was not wasting his time.

* * *

In the completed *Idylls*, the evil in human nature is typified by Saxon heathendom and the beast-infested wilderness. Arthur gains ground against all this. Tennyson embodies the ideal of a spiritually inspired monarchy in an institution that makes a break with medieval romance and the conventions of courtly love. The theme of Soul ruling Body, and keeping the unruly flesh under control, is expressed in Christian marriage. King Arthur thinks it a good thing that his knights should have wives, or, at any rate, virtuous amours with marriage definitely in mind. Some of them do, some at least contemplate matrimony, and the love-affairs of others are, theoretically, 'pure'.

Merlin is a celibate exception. A presence throughout the first half of the cycle, he is central to only one *Idyll*, the story of his downfall – a very Tennysonian downfall. Up to a point he has stood out as a towering 'wisdom' figure and more, Britain's tutelary god once again, in fact; he uses his magic in large-scale public works; he is

---

*See Ashe, *The Discovery of King Arthur* (Stroud; Sutton Publishing, 2005 edn), pp. 83–7, 120–2.

> . . . the most famous man of all those times,
> Merlin, who knew the range of all their arts,
> Had built the King his havens, ships, and halls,
> Was also Bard, and knew the starry heavens.
> *(Merlin and Vivien*, 164–7)

His end comes through a female entanglement, as in earlier versions, but with a change of roles. He is too venerable to be shown lured to disaster by a sexual obsession, at least with any desirable artistic effect. The trouble comes from the woman, Vivien, an unscrupulous schemer who exploits sex for her own ends. She lives at the court among the ladies and damsels, and is tolerated, but hates the knights and has a grudge against Arthur himself for not responding to her advances.

Instead, she sets her sights on Merlin. Behind a display of kittenish frivolity, she has an object that is much more ambitious than seduction. He has mentioned a spell that encloses its victim in a magical prison. Tennyson is following earlier versions, but Vivien's object is to gain power.

> For Merlin once had told her of a charm,
> The which if any wrought on anyone
> With woven paces and with waving arms,
> The man so wrought on ever seem'd to lie
> Closed in the four walls of a hollow tower,
> From which was no escape for evermore.
> . . . And he lay as dead,
> And lost to life and use and name and fame.
> *(Merlin and Vivien*, 203–12)

Vivien wants to inflict this doom on Merlin, in the belief that 'her glory would be great / According to his greatness whom she quench'd.' This is a notion so senseless that it is never explained, but she cherishes it.

Merlin's prophetic foresight warns him that evil days may be coming, as indeed they are, but he does not foresee Vivien contributing to the evil. In a depressed mood he leaves the court and sails over to Brittany. Vivien goes with him, not invited, but not sent home either. He makes for the forest of Broceliande and sits at the foot of a hollow oak (the tree of druidical lore, now empty). Vivien lies down at his feet, though she does not stay in that position. Almost all the rest of this *Idyll* is a dialogue. She talks of love, and flirts, and insinuates herself physically, wrapping Merlin's long beard around her body; his advanced age (Tennyson may be the first to picture him thus, in defiance of his predecessors) makes the relationship more unpleasant.

Flattered, he plays along with her for a while. She manoeuvres the conversation round to the subject of the charm. It doesn't occur to Merlin that she may have designs on him; he says he is afraid that if Vivien knows it, she will use it to trap one of the knights who gossip about her. This brings her resentments into the open.

> What dare the full-fed liars say of me?
> *They* ride abroad redressing human wrongs!
> They sit with knife in meat and wine in horn.
> *They* bound to holy vows of chastity!
> Were I not woman, I could tell a tale.
> (*Merlin and Vivien*, 690–4)

He calls her bluff: can she produce instances of misconduct? She mentions a few scandals which he refutes. From the point of view of a reader today, the passage borders on the comic. One incident is even a thwarted fabliau. She accuses Sir Sagramore of spending an illicit night with one of the girls at court. Merlin says he lost his way in the palace when his torch went out, and wandered into the wrong bedroom. Neither knew the other was there till morning, when they blushed and parted silently, but it was all right because they were 'pure'. 'A likely story,' Vivien comments.

She has a real point with Guinevere and Lancelot, but Merlin refuses to be drawn. Misinterpreting his silence, she pours out invectives against some of the most respected men in King Arthur's circle. This is counter-productive, and it seems certain that Merlin will never tell her what she wants to know. A storm is gathering, and she is about to take her leave, adding:

> If I schemed against thy peace in this,
> May yon just heaven, that darkens o'er me, send
> One flash, that, missing all things else, may make
> My scheming brain a cinder, if I lie.
> (*Merlin and Vivien*, 928–31)

The storm bursts overhead and a nearby tree is struck by lightning. Vivien, in a panic that is still not quite uncalculated, flings herself on Merlin with wild pleas and endearments, and at last she is having some effect:

> The pale blood of the wizard at her touch
> Took gayer colours, like an opal warm'd.

He is tired and confused. He tells her the charm, hardly knowing what he is doing, and falls asleep.

> Then . . . she put forth the charm
> Of woven paces and of waving hands,
> And in the hollow oak he lay as dead,
> And lost to life and use and name and fame.
> Then crying, 'I have made his glory mine,'
> And shrieking out 'O fool!' the harlot leapt
> Adown the forest, and the thicket closed
> Behind her, and the forest echoed 'fool'.
> *(Merlin and Vivien*, 946–72)

Merlin is lost to Arthur and Britain, and his deluded temptress has gained nothing.

The political message of the *Idylls*, to the slight extent that they have one, is not so much that spiritually inspired monarchy might work as that it is the social order best worth trying to make work. The actual conclusion is discouraging. Tragedy prevails. The original glory gives way to gloom. Arthurian morality is sapped, even from above the ordinary sensual level. As Arthur foresees, the Holy Grail ignites inspirations of the wrong kind, and the knights who undertake the Quest are drawn away and unfitted for the duties of their honourable station in life. Also, a far more deadly virus, morality is sapped from below by the sensuality which Merlin's disaster typifies. Guinevere's affair with Lancelot sets a fatal example, and breeds cynicism. Other adulteries and hypocrisies follow, with no excuses admitted. Tristan and Isolde are not spared.

Actually, Tennyson has set himself an insoluble literary problem. The decline of the Round Table is due above all to the royal infidelity, yet, writing in Victoria's reign for a public steeped in its moral atmosphere, he can never describe it. He has to make his characters circle around it and drop hints and show its consequences. There ought to be an Idyll of Lancelot and Guinevere, but there is only an Idyll of Guinevere, alone and guilt-stricken after she has fled to the convent.

Arthur stands firm as everything around him crumbles, but terrible things happen, and now there is no Merlin to foresee and warn. A Red Knight sets up an anarchic and amoral rival court; he is a sort of Hyde to Arthur's Jekyll. Arthur leads a company of knights to suppress him, and they do suppress him, but the attack on his court is a revolting and utterly unchivalrous slaughter. The Red Knight falls to the ground:

> . . . then the knights, who watch'd him, roar'd
> And shouted and leapt down upon the fall'n;
> There trampled out his face from being known,
> And sank his head in mire, and slimed themselves:
> Nor heard the King for their own cries, but sprang
> Thro' open doors, and swording right and left
> Men, women, on their sodden faces, hurl'd
> The tables over and the wines, and slew
> Till all the rafters rang with woman-yells,
> And all the pavement stream'd with massacre.
>
> (*The Last Tournament*, 467–76)

This is the sort of thing that the once noble knighthood has come to.

Meanwhile, in the decline, the old doubts about Arthur's reign have resurfaced, and the scheming Modred can exploit them to launch his revolt. Arthur rides out to meet him with the loyal knights, but on the way he looks in on Guinevere at her convent. He lectures her in several pages of sanctimonious blank verse: she has been the cause of all the trouble by setting a fatal example. The speech is entirely Tennyson's.

The king goes on to his Passing, and in the last *Idyll* Tennyson recovers and achieves some of his finest poetry. He repeats the *Morte d'Arthur* episode with which he began, with further matter before and after. The last battle is a total nightmare, fought at the winter solstice in a 'death white mist'. The battlefield is in Lyonesse, the Cornish territory that has since vanished (significantly) under the waves, Britain's own lost Atlantis. When nearly everyone is dead, Sir Bedivere takes up the wounded king and carries him to a chapel on a 'dark strait of barren land' between the sea and another body of water. Tennyson is probably thinking of, and exaggerating, Loe Bar, a ridge of sand and pebbles separating a long lagoon, Loe Pool, from the sea. Bedivere, at Arthur's reiterated command, casts Excalibur into the water and a hand catches it. Arthur is conveyed away in a boat with a cryptic hope of a Return, which he remembers Merlin holding out. His example survives as a model for others who may attempt the same more successfully.

In 1870–1, during the Franco-Prussian War, Tennyson's work moved closer to public affairs. The papers reported the birth of the third French Republic and the Paris Commune. Tennyson loathed the 'red fool-fury of the Seine', and took the view that French morals had been damaged by the frightful corruption of French literature.

During Victoria's morose retirement, in perpetual mourning for Albert, English republicanism had – for once – become a rising force. The birth of the new republic in France gave it a further impetus, under the leadership of Joseph Chamberlain and Charles Dilke. Then came a reversal. The Prince of Wales, the Queen's eldest son, contracted typhoid and was expected to die. When he recovered, a surge of popular emotion virtually destroyed the anti-royalist movement. In 1872 Tennyson published the *Idylls* in what was almost their final form, with the address to the Queen already quoted, continuing an ardent affirmation of loyalty.

Because of his immense prestige and mass readership, the coincidence was fruitful. A nation receptive to royalism again was presented with the Laureate's vision of Christian monarchy, firmly linked with the Queen and her almost canonised husband. The *Idylls* not only flourished, they made their way into other media. They inspired dramatists and painters; they inspired the pioneer photographer Julia Margaret Cameron, who composed carefully arranged stills illustrating them. Through Tennyson, in fact, Arthur's Britain played an appreciable part in restoring the mystique of the Crown which the four Georges and Victoria's long widowhood had almost effaced.

Tennyson did not, after all, leave Merlin trapped inside the tree. He wrote a final poem, outside the *Idylls* altogether and in a different metre, called 'Merlin and the Gleam'. The speaker in this poem is both Merlin and Tennyson.

O young Mariner,
You from the haven
Under the sea-cliff,
You that are watching
The gray Magician
With eyes of wonder,
I am Merlin,
And *I* am dying,
I am Merlin
Who follow The Gleam.
Mighty the Wizard
Who found me at sunrise
Sleeping, and woke me
And learn'd me Magic!
Great the Master,
And sweet the Magic,
When over the valley
In early summers,
Over the mountain,
On human faces,
And all around me,
Moving to melody
Floated the Gleam . . .

Then, with a melody
Stronger and statelier,
Led me at length
To the city and palace
Of Arthur the king.

As Merlin is both the magician and Tennyson, so Arthur is both the king and Hallam. The two Arthurs, like the two speakers, are indistinguishable, and lines about death and survival apply to both.

> Clouds and darkness
> Closed upon Camelot;
> Arthur had vanish'd
> I knew not whither,
> The king who loved me,
> And cannot die;
> For out of the darkness
> Silent and slowly
> The Gleam, that had waned
>   to a wintry glimmer
> On icy fallow
> And faded forest,
> Drew to the valley
> Named of the shadow,
> And slowly brightening
> Out of the glimmer,
> And slowly moving again
>   to a melody
> Yearningly tender,
> Fell on the shadow,
> No longer a shadow,
> But clothed with The Gleam.
>
> And broader and brighter
> The Gleam flying onward,

Wed to the melody,
Sang thro' the world . . .
And so to the land's
Last limit I come –
And can no longer,
But die rejoicing . . .
There on the border
Of boundless Ocean,
And all but in Heaven,
Hovers The Gleam.

Not of the sunlight,
Not of the moonlight,
Not of the starlight!
O young Mariner,
Down to the haven,
Call your companions,
Launch your vessel,
And crowd your canvas,
And, ere it vanishes
Over the margin,
After it, follow it,
Follow the Gleam.

The Gleam is the highest vision, however conceived. It gives hope, and is to be sought at any cost. Here Tennyson queries the moral of his own *Idylls*, of, at least, the moral most clearly stated in 'The Holy Grail'. There, the highest quest is rejected as right only for the very few, like Galahad. The proper course for ordinary humanity is to stay where God has placed them, and do the work that comes to hand. But the reborn Merlin of this last phase says otherwise. The Quest, or its equivalent, is right, and nothing should be allowed to deter or deflect the seeker. Is Tennyson thinking of the last fourteen lines of Walt Whitman's *Passage to India*? He certainly corresponded with Whitman and had a higher opinion of his poetry than one might suspect.

II

The Merlin Tradition at Home and Overseas

Tennyson's success, besides inspiring Pre-Raphaelite art, also produced effects that might be called literary, with many that might be called sub-literary. Swinburne, reacting against the Laureate's morality, asserted his own in 1882 with a long and intermittently powerful narrative poem, *Tristram of Lyonesse*. Lesser versifiers added their own by-products, most of them not particularly distinguished. There were also compressed versions, popularisations, and introductions to Malory for children, censored and modified in ways suitable for junior readers. The illustrations in books like these were conventionally medieval, and some were hardly even that. One of them had a picture of the single combat between Arthur and the Roman governor Frollo. Arthur wore medieval costume – not even armour – complete with crown; Frollo wore the uniform associated with legionaries in the time of Caesar.

Tennyson's *Idylls* were only accidentally political. Simply because of the number of enthusiasts whom they reached, they played a part in restoring the glamour of the monarchy, and extinguishing English republicanism. While he was writing them, however, a Frenchman was invoking the name of Merlin on behalf of an actual Republic lately extinguished.

Edgar Quinet (1802–75) wrote respected studies of philosophical and religious topics, together with some poetry. He describes in an autobiographical sketch how the French of his youth, still overshadowed by Napoleon and his aftermath, were only gradually discovering new paths. Some opposed the restoration of kings, welcomed the new revolution of 1848 and took a left-wing stance; Quinet was one of these. Others, still not free from the imperial spell, put Napoleon's nephew in power as Napoleon III. Quinet denounced his Second Empire founded on the ruins of the Republic, and was exiled like Victor Hugo, settling in Switzerland. In 1860 he published a counterblast to the Empire in the shape of a long prose allegory, *Merlin l'Enchanteur*, Merlin the Magician. Even apart from the political aspect, the contrast with Tennyson is so extreme as to be almost comic.

Quinet's Merlin, like the Merlin of medieval romance, is the son of a devil – in fact, *the* Devil. But the localisation in Britain disappears, and the break with all accepted versions is soon nearly complete. Merlin is not a Briton even in sympathy; he is, astonishingly, 'the patron of France'. As such, he is the main inspirer of European civilisation, for which, in Quinet's opinion, France has had the largest responsibility.

The story has autobiographical touches, many of which can only be understood fully in the light of notes that Quinet's widow supplied long afterwards. Some familiar characters do appear. In the course of his magical apprenticeship, Merlin visits Taliesin, who recites his famous riddle. Merlin also meets Viviane. She is present at intervals throughout, but never becomes a nemesis, and is generally a sort of Muse for him.

As his reputation grows, rulers seek his advice and friendship. Among them is Arthur, who is in France rather than Britain.

The Enchanter remodels Paris. But he exists on several levels, and his prophetic powers extend beyond ordinary experience. He meets characters who will appear in literature not yet written – Hamlet, Othello, Don Quixote, Juliet, Desdemona, Ophelia, Titania – and discusses their prospects. He enters a limbo inhabited by 'larvae' or phantasms of people destined to make their mark in history, including Charlemagne, Napoleon, Columbus and Michelangelo. Also he goes down to Hell and meets his father. These episodes are entirely foreign to Arthurian legend. If they recall anything, they recall the sixth book of Virgil's *Aeneid* and Dante's *Divine Comedy*. In a rather uncommon touch of humour, Merlin, at the entrance to Hell, meets Virgil himself, who asks him if he is the Florentine whose visit is expected – but no, he isn't. Understandably, people ask him for guidance on matters of religion. He is non-committal, but emphasises one theme: Liberty.

On his travels Merlin acquires a new companion, Jacques Bonhomme. This name was applied in the Middle Ages to peasants who rose against their masters. Merlin's Jacques represents the masses as Quinet sees them, full of ability and goodwill, but liable to be misled. With Jacques's aid, Merlin establishes a French Round Table as a place of assembly for the nations of Europe. Arthur is the most eminent member. He still does not seem to be in Britain, and Merlin's one brief visit to the island has been discouraging. At first Arthur acts as a sort of master of ceremonies, but does not preside. Later in the story he becomes Europe's principal ruler. Dozens of people from western and central Europe, legendary and historical, attend the Round Table, and so do unnamed representatives of countries further afield.

Presently, however, Merlin grows disillusioned. The nations are not making the best use of their opportunities for peace and prosperity. The Grail itself has appeared and yet they are indifferent. He is also having trouble with his father the Devil, who sees him as a rebellious son, too much of an idealist altogether.

Merlin leaves Europe on a prolonged world tour. He returns to find that France and the other nations, lacking his care and protection, have sunk into torpor. The Round Table ceases to be active and Arthur falls into a deathlike sleep. This period of gloom corresponds to the reaction that followed the revolutionary excitements of 1848, and the consequent rise to power of Napoleon III. The people, including Jacques Bonhomme, are corrupted by the meaningless ostentation of the Empire.

Viviane employs the magic which Merlin has taught her to create an enormous tomb for him. The verbal reminiscence here is deceptive. The 'tomb' is a magnificent stronghold, with underground passages branching out through the continent. Merlin lives in it with Viviane, and she bears a son.

At last Arthur awakes, the nations revive, the tyrannies crumble and the story ends on a note of triumph. Merlin is in telegraphic touch with his brother Jonathan across the Atlantic, who symbolises the other great republic. Presumably Quinet is hoping for a new revolution. Merlin's last great enterprise is to convert his father the Devil.

This nineteenth-century political fantasy, which makes Merlin the 'patron of France' and hardly even mentions Britain, can hardly count as belonging to authentic tradition. Quinet, an author of wide interests and concerns, annexed the famous name with a few related motifs to build up a huge, sometimes self-dramatising fiction. It runs to 966 pages in a standard edition. His very French Merlin is, for practical purposes, a different person from the one we know. The fascination that attracted him in the first place remains interesting.

The sub-literature extended to America, and went on for a long time. Booth Tarkington's character Penrod, aged 11, has to take part at school in a sanitised junior pageant of the Round Table. The children sing 'feebly' (Tarkington's word):

> Children of the Table Round,
> Little knights and ladies we,
> Let our voices all resound
> Faith and hope and charitee!

Penrod, as the 'child Sir Lancelot', has to speak of himself inappropriately as 'gentle-hearted, meek and mild'. He is further compelled to say modestly that he is 'but a tot' – a ghastly phrase dictated by the author's need for a rhyme.

━┼━ ⋝◆⋚ ━┼━

Long before Penrod's ordeal, the Tennysonian vogue in America had provoked a leading satirist into a full-scale retort.

Mark Twain (1835–1910) first encountered the Arthurian legend in a junior version, *The Boy's Book of King Arthur*, by Sidney Lanier. He read parts of Malory with admiration, but seems not to have developed any strong interest. However, he knew of the Tennyson-inspired cult of the Middle Ages, and disapproved. He began writing *A Connecticut Yankee in King Arthur's Court* in 1884, then set it aside, and finished it only in 1889. A congenial illustrator, Dan Beard, made his maliciously conceived Merlin look like Tennyson. The novel has been filmed several times, and Rodgers and Hart made a musical of it (*A Connecticut Yankee*, 1927).

Twain's *Connecticut Yankee* is a curious mixture of straightforward comedy, satire on romantic medievalism, and somewhat confused moralising. The narrator, Hank Morgan, is a factory superintendent who knows everything about manufacturing (especially the manufacture of weapons) and not much about anything else. Stunned by a blow on the head, he finds himself in King Arthur's England. It has a different chronology. The year is 528, just possible for a hypothetical 'historical' Arthur, but absurd for the Arthurian England of romance; a date, however, is needed for the story, as is soon evident. Hank is conducted under guard to the court, where he sees some of the principal legendary characters, including Merlin. The wizard is 'a very old and white-bearded man, clothed in a long black gown'. He is regarded as a 'mighty liar and magician', and a bore, but he is influential because he is supposed to have power over storms, lightning and evil spirits. He becomes hostile to Hank and remains so.

Hank saves himself from possible execution by a prodigious feat of magic, or what the court accepts as such. Aware from the date that an eclipse is imminent, he announces that he will darken the sun, and when the eclipse happens the impact is overwhelming. Hank is treated with reverent awe and is soon given almost dictatorial powers. He adopts a title, calling himself 'the Boss'. Henceforth he is, in effect, the kingdom's new Merlin, a scientific and technological Merlin, putting the old one in the shade. It is clear that the old Merlin cannot compete, since he is hardly more than a conjuror exploiting superstition. His hostility to the Connecticut Yankee remains implacable.

Hank learns to respect King Arthur and some of the knights. But his attitude to most of the people, as shown in his narrative, is condescending at best. He sneers at the knights themselves for their futile 'grailing', without bothering to discuss what the Grail Quest may be about or why it is futile, and he writes verbatim reports of conversations with humbler persons, designed to prove that they are too stupid to follow a simple argument.

Twain's contrast between the old and the new, nearly always weighted in favour of the new, might be expected to convey a clear message to the reader. Actually the message transmitted through Hank becomes less clear as the story proceeds. The reader can easily feel that the best things in it are (as might be expected) the passages of straight humour, such as Hank's exasperated account of the difficulty and discomfort of wearing medieval armour on a hot day. And the reader might be excused for thinking so: the author's own 1883 notebook reveals that the armour problem was the germ of the novel. Its more ideological and pretentious elements came later.

If the comedy is the best feature of *Connecticut Yankee*, the worst, going beyond Hank's sniping at individuals, is his broader determination to show modern man's superiority, by contrast with the servility and stagnation that most of Arthur's subjects live in. For this, he lays most of the blame on the all-powerful Church. Sometimes the contrasts are effective, even amusing. Sometimes they are not amusing at all, as when Hank (or Mark Twain speaking through Hank) rightly denounces tyranny and oppression – he finds plenty of both in Arthur's kingdom – but exaggerates the horrors beyond credibility.

With all Hank's confidence as the new Merlin, it becomes harder and harder to see where he is going. He improves the kingdom with innovations such as printing and railways, and begins to plan democratic reforms. But he does it all by handing down orders from above, without building popular support. Arthur is killed fighting the rebel Mordred. With his authority gone, Hank's activities lead to conflict, especially with the Church; and in a showdown, the Church is bound to have the support of the majority. The Boss and a few followers confront the knights and a host of other dissidents, whereupon the morality of the story turns upside down. He applies his knowledge of explosives and electricity to slaughter his opponents, more than twenty-five thousand of them in a couple of days, without compunction. So, after all, modern man is not better than the people to whom progress is supposed to have made him superior. He is worse. 'We fifty-four', says Hank complacently, 'were masters of England.' Only a little while ago, he was talking of giving England democracy.

The end of the story is told by one of the few, trapped in the middle of a mass of corpses. The Boss is wounded and asleep. And now the Arthurian world strikes back, in the person of Merlin, whose magic turns out not to be wholly fraudulent. He arrives shaved and disguised as a woman, offering help, and gains access to the oblivious Boss, whom he throws into a trance that will go on for more than a thousand years of 'alternative' time. At last, when this has caught up with the nineteenth century, the trance will end and Hank will be himself again.

Mark Twain believed that he was raising serious issues in this book, and so, intermittently, he was. But talking with Dan Beard, his illustrator, he partially repudiated his own creation: 'This Yankee of mine has neither the refinement nor weakness of a college education; he is a perfect ignoramus; he is boss of a machine shop; he can build a locomotive or a Colt's revolver, he can put up and run a telegraph line, but he's an ignoramus, nevertheless.' Perhaps it is reassuring to know that.

In spite of Mark Twain, it was an American poet who carried the Tennyson tradition into the twentieth century. Edwin Arlington Robinson (1869–1935) was born in Maine and attended Harvard University. He held several jobs, the only one of interest being at the Customs Office in New York, to which he was appointed by Theodore Roosevelt. He resigned from this post after four years and devoted himself to writing.

His *Collected Poems* won a Pulitzer prize in 1922. Some, such as *Richard Corey*, are established anthology pieces. He also wrote three long narrative poems on Arthurian subjects. Robinson's blank verse is sometimes reminiscent of Tennyson's, but never imitative. His originality consists more in reinterpreting old themes than in inventing new ones. The first of the three poems is *Merlin*, which appeared in 1917 during the First World War, and reflects some of the grief and disillusionment of the time. After it came *Lancelot* in 1920 and *Tristram* in 1927; *Tristram* won another Pulitzer prize.

Robinson's Merlin is not a magician, but he does have a prophetic gift, besides being extremely intelligent and, in his relations with men in power, statesmanlike. He is ageing, but not old. As in Tennyson Arthur's kingdom is drifting toward decay, but Merlin is away in the Breton forest of Broceliande, where he and Vivian are happy. There is no hint of betrayal here; they love each other, and Robinson portrays her with sympathy.

Temporarily back in Britain, Merlin renews his acquaintance with the king. It does not appear that he can render any service by staying. He returns to Broceliande, where he is free to settle into a pleasant and permanent retirement. However, as disturbing reports reach him, it becomes an insistent question whether this would be a dereliction of duty. His loyalty is not extinct. Finally he does go back to Britain, and witnesses the ruin of Camelot.

This reappearance of a long-absent Merlin, at the end of the Arthurian saga, is exceptional. Usually he remains in whatever trap or retreat has received him. However, he also reappears at the end – though very differently – in the original version of T.H. White's multiple novel *The Once and Future King*.

12

The New Matter of Britain

L ast of the pure traditionalists was Terence Hanbury White (1906–64), author of *The Once and Future King*. That title translates the phrase *Rex quondam rexque futurus*, said to have been inscribed on Arthur's tomb at Glastonbury. White was a solitary man with a deep dislike of the times he lived in, and a vast fund of out-of-the-way knowledge – knowledge of animals, for instance, and outdoor sports including falconry. A pacifist in outlook, he was tormented by the state of the world, yet he never lost his ebullient sense of humour.

In 1937 he brought out the first of his Arthurian tales, *The Sword in the Stone*. He achieved originality at one bound by exploring an aspect of the legend that almost everyone else ignored: Arthur's boyhood and education. Spenser had introduced the theme, but so differently that White's treatment stood alone, unrivalled.

Arthur's education is in the hands of his tutor Merlin, who is, superficially, quite like the post-Tennysonian ancient wizard with beard and robe. He is based to some extent on the author himself, and is made more of an independent creation by the spelling 'Merlyn'. Some of his familiar features are present, but transformed. He is a prophet, as ever, but his gift is topsy-turvy: he remembers the future and forgets the past. While much of his pupil's education is fairly formal, the most important parts are magical. Merlyn changes the boy – who is called 'the Wart', never 'Arthur', till the last page – into a series of animals, so that he can experience life and its hazards in a variety of forms. His evocations of what it would be like to undergo a magical working are among the most ingenious things in his repertoire.

The boy wants to be a fish, and it happens.

He found that he had tumbled off the drawbridge, landing with a smack on his side in the water. He found that the moat and the bridge had grown hundreds of times bigger. He knew that he was turning into a fish.

(Into a perch, in fact.)

'Oh, Merlyn,' he cried, 'Please come too.'

'For this once,' said a large and solemn tench beside his ear. 'But in future you will have to go by yourself. Education is experience.' . . .

The Wart found it difficult to be a new kind of creature. It was no good trying to swim like a human being, for it made him go corkscrew and much too slowly. . . .

'Not like that,' said the tench in ponderous tones. 'Put your chin on your left shoulder and do jack-knives. Never mind about the fins to begin with.'

The Wart's legs had fused together into his backbone and his feet and toes had become a tail fin. His arms had become two more fins . . . of a delicate pink.

When he has had some practice, he looks around at a different universe.

For one thing, the heavens or sky above him was now a perfect circle. The horizon had closed to this. In order to imagine yourself into the Wart's position, you would have to picture a round horizon, a few inches about your head, instead of the flat horizon which you usually see. Under this horizon of air you would have to imagine another horizon of under water, spherical and practically upside down – for the surface of the water acted partly as a mirror to what was below it. It is difficult to imagine. What makes it a great deal more difficult to imagine is that everything which human beings would consider to be above the water level was fringed with all the colours of the spectrum.

Later comes a conversation with a pike.

The Wart . . . hardly noticed that the tight mouth was coming closer and closer to him. It came imperceptibly . . . and suddenly it was looming within an inch of his nose. On the last sentence it opened, horrible and vast, the skin stretching ravenously from bone to bone and tooth to tooth. Inside there seemed to be nothing but teeth. . . . It was only at the last second that he was able to regain his own will, to pull himself together, to recollect his instructions and to escape. All those teeth clashed behind him at the tip of his tail.

After much equally vivid education, *The Sword in the Stone* ends when the Wart extracts the sword and becomes King Arthur. White, however, did not see this as the conclusion. He contracted with his publishers, Collins, to write three further novels covering Arthur's reign, along the lines laid down by

Malory. Unlike the first book, the later ones have never been thought acceptable as children's classics. Besides amatory and political matter, they include touches of curious gruesomeness. Nevertheless they are still abundantly entertaining.

As presented by White, the realm of Arthurian romance is no longer quasi-historical or pseudo-historical; it is completely and deliberately divorced from history. Merlyn's multiple time-scale becomes thematic. The reader is pitched into a sort of ideal universe where the entire panorama of the Middle Ages is present at once. White occasionally mentions real monarchs, such as Henry III of England and Louis XI of France, but he speaks of them as fictitious. They are mere shadows; the realm of King Arthur is the substance. He goes further, not simply rejecting history but inverting it. The original Arthur would have been Celtic, but White's is an English Plantagenet with Saxon serfs, and the Celts are his enemies.

In spite of radical departures like these, White minimised his originality, claiming that he was merely following Malory and inventing very little. Not so. He gives a fresh life even to the familiar characters, developing them legitimately, and sometimes giving the impression that nobody is ever likely to develop them further. Moreover, he has a rare talent for picking out hints and building them up. The Saracen knight Palomides talks like an Indian who has learned English but does not speak it as his own language. The absurdly questing knight Pellinore, clearly the product of an English public school, achieves a long-delayed and ironic success. Elaine is perpetually *de trop* and inept. And White, unlike earlier authors, faces the difficulties inherent in the Round Table. Merlyn uses the formula $2\pi r$ to prove that a table for a hundred and fifty knights would be impracticably enormous.

White hardly ever mentions academic theories about a 'historical Arthur'. They are irrelevant, and he is contemptuous of them. Arthur, he says, was not a 'distressed Briton hopping about in a suit of woad in the fifth century'. The search for a historical basis belongs, in his eyes, to our modern, unknightly, iconoclastic world. Towards the end he allows this world to break into the story with a shocking impact, shattering his wonderful sphere of imagination at a precise moment during Mordred's revolt.

> 'Mordred is using guns.'
> Rochester asked in bewilderment: 'Guns?'
> 'He is using the cannon.'
> It was too much for the old priest's intellects.
> 'It is incredible!' he said. 'To say we are dead, and to marry the queen! And then to use cannon. . . .'
> 'Now that the guns have come,' said Arthur, 'the Table is over. We must hurry home.'
> 'To use cannons against men!'

White could have made the point with that one dreadful moment of revelation. However, his personal convictions were already intruding. In the later parts of his work he was involving ideals of cosmopolitanism and pacifism, and trying to make the chivalry of the Round Table foreshadow them. It could not. He wrote an additional book, in which Merlyn reappeared on the eve of Arthur's last battle, and resumed the lessons of his boyhood in a sombre spirit, inappropriately. He used an ant-hill to give a warning against totalitarianism which Arthur could not have understood. White regarded this fifth book as an antidote to war. His publishers took a different view. It was outside the terms of the contract. The atmosphere was all wrong, and under the current war-time restrictions the intended one-volume edition of the four novels could not absorb a fifth; the cost and complications would be prohibitive. So *The Once and Future King* attained its final form as a tetralogy.

White was unwilling to surrender completely. Revising *The Sword in the Stone* for its place at the beginning of the one-volume edition, he made cuts that eliminated several of the best passages, and put in some of the material he had written for the fifth book. The result was infelicitous. *The Sword in the Stone* remains brilliant, but it is best read in its original form. The manuscript of the aborted fifth book came into the possession of the University of Texas. After much hesitation it was published separately in 1977 as *The Book of Merlyn*.

When T.H. White wrote, the position that he maintained, together with other forms of Arthurian traditionalism, was being undermined. Arthurian history – or possible history – was percolating in. The wide readership of Tennyson's *Idylls* had other effects. It created Arthurian 'traditions' that were not really traditional. People who knew of local legends, however vaguely, wanted to connect them with Arthur. Hence, for instance, the enduring reputation of Dozmary Pool, in the bleak heart of Bodmin Moor, about 900 feet above sea-level. The Pool is reached by a minor road that branches off from the main highway near Jamaica Inn, well known through Daphne du Maurier's novel. It is one of the places – there are six – where Sir Bedivere is said to have cast Excalibur into the water, with Arthur dying nearby.

Dozmary Pool is undoubtedly atmospheric. In winter the mist can hide the opposite shore, giving the impression of a much larger expanse of water. However, it is not near any alleged site of Camlann, Arthur's last battle. Its sombre reputation may be due to a legend that actually is associated with it, about the sinister ghost of Jan Tregeagle (pronounced Tregayle), a cruel and corrupt magistrate. He was condemned posthumously, as penance, to perform impossible tasks, one of them being to bail out Dozmary Pool with a leaking limpet shell. The notion may have been suggested by an old rumour that the Pool was bottomless. (In fact in 1859 it dried up and was seen to be shallow.)

Merlin is not connected with Dozmary Pool, but he does appear at another famous place, where, as with Dozmary's Arthur, his modern presence is probably a post-Tennysonian fancy, yet intriguing all the same. The tale told at Alderley Edge in Cheshire is one of several about hidden caves where Arthur lies asleep, perhaps accompanied by his knights. The oldest known legend of this type belongs, appropriately, to Cadbury Castle in Somerset, the reputed original of Camelot. Another, recorded by Sir Walter Scott, concerns the Eildon Hills near Melrose in the Border country. Another is told of Craig-y-Ddinas in Glamorgan. At both Melrose and Craig-y-Ddinas a mysterious stranger conducts someone into the cave. The Alderley Edge version is similar.

A few miles from Macclesfield the ground falls away sharply to the Cheshire plain. The Edge is on the north side of a sandstone ridge that runs through woods clinging to a steep slope. The path along it goes under outcroppings of mossy rock, and passes a place where water drips from the rock into a stone trough.

Once upon a time, the story goes, a farmer was on his way to the market at Macclesfield, riding a white mare which he hoped to sell. On the ridge-road a grey-bearded man stopped him and offered to buy her. The farmer thought his offer too low, and rode on. At the market the mare was admired but no purchaser came forward, so the farmer remounted to go home. The bearded man stopped him again and made a fresh offer. He led the farmer through the woods on the Edge, and laid his hand on a rock, which moved, revealing a pair of gates. They walked through into a cave. 'In this cave,' the stranger said, 'Arthur and his knights lie asleep till their country needs them. Their horses are with them, but they are one short. Will you sell yours now?' He held out a purse of gold. The farmer snatched it and ran out of the cave in terror. The gates clashed shut behind him and the rock returned to its normal position. Of course no one has ever found it since.

The story may have been inspired partly by real caves further down the slope, and by folk-memories of Roman copper mines. Today the horse purchaser is identified as Merlin, in some strange form of immortality. This may not always have been so, but his annexation would have been a natural consequence of post-Tennysonian fancy. The trough counts as a wishing well. Above it is an inscription cut deep in the rock:

DRINK OF THIS AND TAKE THY FILL FOR THE
WATER FALLS BY THE WIZARDS WILL

The letters are not ancient in style. Above the word DRINK a face is carved, which is more heavily weathered than the lettering, and may be older.

Serious historical speculation began quietly as far back as 1927 with *Midsummer Night*, a group of tales in verse by John

Masefield, who became Poet Laureate. In one of the poems, 'Badon Hill', he imagined a battle between Britons led by Arthur and Saxon pirates raiding up the rivers into the west of Britain, a battle as it might actually have been. Masefield's poetic initiative was not followed up, but in 1936, in the first volume of the *Oxford History of England* (now superseded), R.G. Collingwood proposed a theory about events in post-Roman Britain that attracted lasting interest. He suggested that the Britons had been able to turn the tide temporarily against the Saxons by the use of heavy cavalry on the late Roman model, to which the pedestrian invaders had no answer. Arthur, on this showing, would have been an imperial-type cavalry commander, rather than a king. This interpretation appealed to many who recognised that Geoffrey of Monmouth and the romancers could not be trusted for facts, but were glad to find a real person behind their fiction, and even to find prototypes for the knights in Arthur's hypothetical horsemen.

Collingwood's theory, popularisations of it and much-publicised archaeological projects, led to the gradual growth of a new interest in the 'historical Arthur' question. Some traditionalists objected, as White did. The objection ran roughly thus: 'We have the Arthurian stories, which are immortal literature. Looking for the historical facts behind them is a mistake. At best it is irrelevant, at worst it spoils the stories by contrasting them with a smaller and duller reality.'

The answer became apparent. The historical quest was not adverse to the mythos, it enlarged and enriched it. It inspired a succession of new writers who built up what might fairly be called a New Matter of Britain.

The first, whose voice was heard quite soon after Collingwood's, was the novelist and poet Charles Williams. He was one of the Oxford circle that became famous as the Inklings: in retrospect, the best known of them were C.S. Lewis and J.R.R. Tolkien. Williams's two small books, *Taliessin through Logres* and *The Region of the Summer Stars*, together composed a cycle of complex poems that introduced themes and characters from Arthurian romance, but added others, and imagined a context in a post-Roman Britain abandoned by the emperors and set on its feet again by Arthur. Williams also wrote part of a general discussion of Arthurian literature, including quasi-historical aspects. After his death, C.S. Lewis combined the fragment with a commentary of his own on the poems, and published the result as *Arthurian Torso*. Lewis took the same Collingwood-style view of the 'historical Arthur'.

Lewis himself wrote three novels comprising a *Cosmic Trilogy*, in the third of which, *That Hideous Strength* (1945), the historical issue is briefly aired again, and Merlin makes a spectacular appearance. The principal character appears in all three. He is Elwin Ransom, a philologist and a Fellow of a Cambridge college. For complicated reasons he visits both Mars and Venus. Besides learning about the inhabitants (in the 1940s inhabitants could still be allowed), he encounters the Higher Powers – archons or angels – who are associated with the planets he visits. A long time ago, he is told, the corresponding Earth-spirit 'fell', blasted the Moon into desolation and inaugurated the terrestrial reign of evil. From the point of view of the solar system, Earth has been closed off ever since, the 'Silent Planet'.

That Hideous Strength happens on Earth. Its focus is an organisation called the National Institute of Co-ordinated Experiments (NICE), which is supposed to be carrying out research for the benefit of humanity. This, however, is only a front. NICE is actually run by a core group with a hidden agenda. They are planning mass exterminations and other atrocities, with the aim of creating an elitist technocratic society, and NICE's money, influence and expert public relations enable them to prepare with a free hand. To some extent they foreshadow the Inner Party in Orwell's *Nineteen Eighty-Four* (written later). However, there is one crucial difference. They accept the existence of non-material realities, and try to ally themselves with formidable beings – which they call 'macrobes' so as to sound scientific – who belong to the realm of the fallen Earth-spirit. In effect, NICE is in the hands of diabolists. Dr Ransom, together with a small group, is the only human being who understands what is going on.

For some reason that is not very clear, Merlin comes back to life. The diabolists believe, rightly, that he embodies an immensely ancient magic that can be reinvigorated. Not knowing anything of his morality, they fancy that he will help them. Fortunately they mistake a tramp for the revived magician, and waste time talking to him in different languages, none of which he understands.

Meanwhile the real Merlin arrives at Ransom's house and asks him three obscure questions which he answers correctly, as no one could without having undergone his cosmic experiences. Satisfied as to his credentials, Merlin accepts that NICE must be defeated, but does not know how. Ransom, however, does know that the diabolists, by opening a channel to the spiritual realm, have also opened a way for the planetary powers to enter the Silent Planet. The enemy will be destroyed: they have 'pulled down Deep Heaven on their heads'. Merlin becomes the catalyst for the invasion, and NICE collapses, in a confusion recalling the Tower of Babel.

At a mundane level the most interesting aspect of Lewis's reconstitution of Merlin is his attempt to imagine what he would be like as a person, how present-day people would regard him, and how he would respond to a modern environment. He talks fifth-century Latin, using words that might be puzzling to a Classical scholar. When he bursts in through Ransom's front door, he is domineering: the occupants of the house are (in his eyes) so poorly dressed that he takes them for servants and demands to see the Master. Ransom calms him down. He notices, as others do, that Merlin eats without using forks, yet seems elegant; it isn't a case of his having no manners but of his having different ones. His reactions to other domestic matters are mixed:

'I cannot understand the way you live and your house is strange to me. You give me a bath such as the Emperor himself might envy, but no one attends me to it; a bed softer than sleep itself, but when I rise from it I find I must put on my own clothes with my own hands as if I were a peasant. I lie in a room with windows of pure crystal so that you can see the sky as clearly when they are shut as when they are open, and there is not wind enough within the room to blow out an unguarded taper; but I lie in it alone with no more honour than a prisoner in a dungeon. Your people eat dry and tasteless flesh but it is off plates as smooth as ivory and as round as the sun. In all the house there are warmth and softness and silence that might put a man in mind of paradise terrestrial; but no hangings, no beautified pavements, no musicians, no perfumes, no high seats, not a gleam of gold, not a hawk, not a hound. You seem to me to live neither like a rich man nor a poor one.'

When Ransom convinces him that NICE is a menace, he still cannot understand its nature, or grasp why there is no established authority capable of exposing or checking it. He remembers Arthur and his triumphs over the Saxons. Admittedly Arthur has gone, but is there nothing else to oppose the evil? Nothing, says Ransom. The Church is feeble and fragmented. Kings (including the current one, George VI) are ineffectual. There is no Emperor. . . . That last negation is the one that really gives Merlin pause, as a man conditioned by centuries of imperial rule with no alternative. It is this awareness of a totally different society that forces him to comply with Ransom's apocalyptic argument.

That Hideous Strength is not primarily Arthurian, but in Lewis's characterisation of Merlin, and the attendant discussions, the New Matter of Britain is continuing to emerge. Within a few years the books start to appear. The first of them conform, more or less, to the view of Arthur laid down by Collingwood and those who agreed with him, including Williams and Lewis. Later ones increasingly go their own way, but keep the grip on history which Collingwood pioneered.

Alfred Duggan, a writer hampered in his youth by excessive wealth, escaped from an alcoholic haze into honourable war service, and retired in his forties to produce historical novels set in various periods. They are lucid, accurate and well informed without an overload of learning. *Conscience of the King* (1951) takes the form of a first-person narrative by Cerdic, the leader of the West Saxons and ancestor of subsequent English royalty. Arthur is glimpsed at a distance with his cavalry force, and encountered once in a single explosive clash: he is the only Briton whom Cerdic learns to be afraid of. *Sword at Sunset* (1963), by Rosemary Sutcliff, is an attempt to present Arthur full-length as the Britons' war-leader. Rosemary Sutcliff, hitherto a writer of children's books, makes Arthur tell the story himself. This was felt by some to be an over-audacious thing for a woman to attempt, but the result justified her. *Sword at Sunset* remains a minor classic, well planned, well researched and well told.

One major novelist was on the cusp of the transition, though he made no contribution to it himself. The Nobel Laureate John Steinbeck testified to the importance of Malory in his childhood reading, as early as the age of 9. The effect does not show in his greater novels, such as *The Grapes of Wrath*, but it does, if unobtrusively, in one or two of the others. Steinbeck claimed that the influence was present in *Tortilla Flat*, and tried to convey this by his preface and chapter headings, though not very convincingly; and the alleged Arthurian motifs in *Of Mice and Men* and *Cannery Row* are even less evident. However, his Arthurian fascination was real. It led him to take a continuing interest in Malory and to try to translate him into a modern idiom.

The result, published after his death, was entitled *The Acts of King Arthur and his Noble Knights*. It is a retelling rather than a translation, as Steinbeck's reputation might lead the reader to expect. His published correspondence about Arthurian literature is more interesting than the book itself. But while he was occupied with it, he was also discovering the 'historical Arthur' question, and making non-academic investigations of his own. He lived in Somerset for a while, looked about and speculated. He did not recoil as White did.

Cadbury-Camelot naturally drew his attention, even before the excavations that began in 1966. As secretary of the project, I was in touch with him. I had heard of his interest, and asked

him if there was any truth in a rumour that he had planned a
new book in the Arthurian field and then abandoned it because
of something he had been reading – a matter for regret, if so.
He replied courteously and at some length, denying the
rumour, and going on to offer ideas of his own. I invited him to
visit the Cadbury site, but sadly he was too ill and died soon
afterwards. If he had made the visit, a distinguished
contribution to the New Matter of Britain would very likely
have resulted.

As it was, he gave me an account of his own amateur
excavations on a Somerset hill near Evercreech, where badgers
abounded. His 'badger method' consisted in taking a shovel to
the badger's sett when the animal was at home, and shovelling
earth into it. The badger, alarmed, would try to dig his way out
and throw up piles of earth. Steinbeck then sifted through it
and found Roman coins and other interesting objects. Did he
really do this? My suspicion at the time was that the technique
was a joke on his part, but an archaeologist in Wisconsin – the
Badger State – assured me that the method has actually been
used.

These authors added nothing significant to the conception of
Merlin himself. But Rosemary Sutcliff had shown, in *Sword at
Sunset*, that Arthur's story could be told as a first-person
narrative, and told, moreover, by a woman without being
damned by male prejudice. It followed that the same could be
done with Merlin, and Mary Stewart did it.

She was a successful writer of contemporary fiction before
she turned her attention to the Matter of Britain. Her first
Merlin book, *The Crystal Cave* (1970), is presented as a

reminiscence by Merlin long after the events. The writing is so vivid and imaginative that the novel gives an impression of being more original than it is. Essentially this is Geoffrey of Monmouth restructured, reinterpreted and elaborated. The principal change is that Merlin has a normal paternity as an illegitimate son of Ambrosius Aurelianus, the British military leader whom Geoffrey converts into 'King Aurelius Ambrosius'. Merlin is a seer, and serves Ambrosius and Uther in that capacity, but he is not a magician, though he acquires an ambiguous reputation. He conserves and reinforces his gift by sexual restraint.

The 'cave' of the title is suggested by the legends of Merlin's Hill near Carmarthen. In the Dinas Emrys episode, he reveals the pool and makes extempore use of a banner and a shooting star to awe everyone with talk about dragon omens. He transports one sacred stone from Ireland to Stonehenge – only one – and sets it up over Ambrosius's grave. He contrives Uther's entry into Tintagel Castle by a disguise, aided by complicity on Ygerna's part, though, when the news is brought of her husband's death, Uther is (to put it mildly) unappreciative – the contrivance was unnecessary, and he could soon have got access to Gorlois's widow and married her. He has no use for the imminent son who is taken away; but the son, whose future Merlin foresees, is Arthur.

Mary Stewart's next Merlin novel, *The Hollow Hills* (1973), is very different and bears the imprint of further reading. She covers the same ground as *The Sword in the Stone*, Arthur's youth with Merlin as his protector, culminating in his accession; but in a way that is not White's way, or even her own in her first book. She leaves Geoffrey of Monmouth behind and moves into a kind of intuitive history of her own in a milieu of 'confusion and seeking', though without losing touch with real history. The hollow hills are points of contact between this world and the Celtic Otherworld, with which Merlin can communicate. Referring in an Author's Note to this inscrutable time, she speaks of a 'multiplicity of vision', and generously quotes some observations of my own in a book written long ago, *From Caesar to Arthur*. Since she chooses this passage as a fair statement of what she wishes to say, and I still think it is not too badly put, I feel justified in repeating it here.

When Christianity prevailed and Celtic paganism crumbled into mythology, a great deal of this sort of thing was carried over. Water and islands retained their magic. Lake-spirits flitted to and fro, heroes travelled in strange boats. The haunted hills became fairy-hills, belonging to vivid fairy folk hardly to be paralleled among other nations. . . . Unseen realms intersected the visible, and there were secret means of communication and access. The fairies and the heroes, the ex-gods and the demi-gods, jostled the spirits of the dead, in kaleidoscopic confusion. . . . Everything grew ambiguous. Thus, long after the triumph of Christianity, there continued to be fairy-hills. . . . There were saints of whom miracles were reported; but similar miracles, not long since, might have been the business of fully identifiable gods. There were glass castles where a hero might lie an age entranced; there were blissful fairylands to be reached by water or by cave-passageways. . . . Journeys and enchantments, combats and imprisonments – theme by theme the Celtic imagination articulated itself in story. Yet any given episode might be taken as fact or imagination or religious allegory or all three at once.

In the second novel one theme combines the mystical and the material. This is the quest for a physical object with profound associations, the sword of the Emperor Maximus, a figure from the Roman past who is also a hero of British legend. When the sword is found, Merlin gives it to Arthur as a token of power, long predestined. Hostility comes from the sinister Morgause, Arthur's half-sister, the mother of the evil Mordred. The third novel, *The Last Enchantment* (1979), shows Merlin still exerting his influence over Arthur's reign and enduring the machinations of Morgause. The atmosphere, however, is quieter. Merlin's love for Nimue, the woman who entraps him in some of the romances, is harmless here and even idyllic. He goes into retirement for a time, but voluntarily. Nimue becomes, in some degree, his successor.

Mary Stewart's narration and characterisation are among the best in the field. I was once privileged to conduct her and her husband over the Cadbury hill – a privilege, alas, that I never experienced with John Steinbeck.

Four further novelists deserve attention: Marion Zimmer Bradley, previously known as a writer of science fiction; Parke Godwin; Persia Woolley; and Bernard Cornwell. These and other novelists have all succeeded in weaving together history, literature and imagination. Two of them have experimented, in their own way, with existing elements in the Merlin tradition. Marion Bradley recognises the possibility of several Merlins, perhaps in a series, though one may be pre-eminent at a given time. Parke Godwin dismisses imagery of age and makes Merlin a boy, as he is at the beginning of his adventures.*

* See further the Appendix.

Note

In recent years the 'historical Arthur' has been undergoing a certain decline. This has been due mainly to a barrage of academic scepticism (to employ a polite term that is not always the most descriptive). If Arthur is on his way out, perhaps the phenomenon I have called the New Matter of Britain is nearing its end.

Literary anticipation, however, is always unwise, and the debunking of the historical Arthur is inconclusive. It has been due largely to scholars asking the wrong questions, following futile lines of argument and inevitably reaching a dead end. But other lines do exist, and one of them, I believe, does lead to a documented person in the fifth century, who is acceptable as the starting-point of the legend – whether or not you call him the 'historical Arthur'. The main case has been before the public for a long time, and, so far as I know, has never been effectively faulted by anyone who has studied it carefully and impartially. Through this and through its ramifications, if in no other way, new fiction, films, or whatever, may emerge. At present I do not find any relevance to Merlin.

See Ashe, *The Discovery of King Arthur* (Stroud: Sutton Publishing, 2003) and Christopher Snyder, *Exploring the World of King Arthur* (London, Thames & Hudson, 2000).

Epilogue:
Merlin's Island

Even a modest sampling of the literature is enough to show that Merlin can be fictionalised, and theorised about, in a whole variety of ways, from ridicule to apotheosis. As an attempt to sum him up, so far as that is possible, I repeat a few sentences which I wrote when considering him before.*

In Merlin's principal manifestations, apart from satiric ones like Mark Twain's, he may be said to embody *Something Else*. Something that is not simply unusual but radically Other. [Here I mentioned C.S. Lewis's Dr Dimble, quoted above, and proceeded.]

Merlin makes prophecies of the future, like speculative Christians, but they have little in common with pious daydreaming about the Second Coming or the End of the World. He works magic, but he does it purposefully, in a long-term programme for Britain and its king; he is not a mere fairy-tale trickster, much less is he a Faust pursuing his own ends. He conforms to a Christian society, yet he is often close to the world of pagan mythology. His only specific Christian activity is to prepare the way for the Grail

* Ashe, *Merlin* (Newton Toney: Wessex Books, 2001), p. 28.

Quest, and this, though Christian-inspired, has no place in traditional belief or legend.

In his mythic fullness he is an unclassifiable being with unique powers and knowledge, neither divine nor demonic, yet with something of both – human despite his profound strangeness, and supportive of the good, if in ways that are no one else's.

One thing I am clear about is that Merlin must not be approached by way of abstraction and sophistication. He is not, as critics have argued, the archetypal 'Wise Old Man' of Jungian psychology, if only because he is not a Wise Old Man. He is more interesting than that. In his primary career he is, first, a precocious child; then, a disconcerting youth; and later, a mature royal counsellor – old perhaps from the viewpoint of the Lake damsel who traps him, but not chronologically old, and, in that fatal lapse, far from wise. He does become old in versions influenced by Tennyson, but even then the entrapment calls his wisdom in question, as Tennyson made very clear in his 'Vivien' story.

The long summer of Merlin's ascendancy, before his downfall, is marvellous enough without any archetypes intruding. Medieval authors relate this enigmatic person to the legends of his strange birth. Because of the replacement of a human father by a more-than-human entity, Merlin is only partly human himself, and has preternatural powers and a mysterious link with a spirit that takes control of him.

Moreover, he is not a mere random thaumaturge. He has one unique attribute which his origin entirely fails to explain. In the mainstream as defined by Geoffrey and Malory (not of course the later developments) he is devoted to the interests of Britain.

Given his fifth-century context, 'patriotism' may not be quite the word for his commitment, but it is something like that.

He arrives on the scene denouncing the traitor Vortigern and dropping the first hints of a national deliverer. He raises a monument honouring the victims of Vortigern's Saxon friends. He establishes Britain's special status in Christendom, through possession of the Grail, and causes the Round Table to be made as a symbolic link with Christ and a meeting-place for the anticipated knighthood. He contrives Arthur's birth, and removes him to a safe haven of concealment till the time comes for him to reign. He sets the stage for the test that enthrones the young prince as Britain's king. Without fighting himself, he helps Arthur to conquer his enemies, and provides him, by mysterious means, with his all-subduing weapon. Then he does the one thing that is not inspired by his British dedication – and it has catastrophic results. His amorous involvement takes him away, and with Merlin gone the kingdom begins a slow slide downhill.

It is worth asking whether a true parallel can be found anywhere else. History commemorates individuals as patriots and national heroes; religion recognises celestial patron saints, watching over particular countries. But does any mythology include a character who is human, yet as much more-than-human as Merlin is; who would count as a god or demigod in a non-Christian culture; and who lives on earth single-mindedly committed to the good of the country he makes his home, and the glory and prosperity of its ruler, who is his own creation?

I have wondered whether Hinduism offers a parallel in Krishna. He is an avatar of the Supreme God Vishnu in the shape of an earthly prince, and he plays a decisive part in the epic *Mahabharata*. This is centred on a dynastic conflict between two branches of a royal house in northern India, the Pandavas who are the 'good' side and the Kauravas who are 'bad'. The Pandavas' leader, Yudhishthir, is the rightful king, but the Kauravas' leader Duryodhana tricks him into resigning and going into exile with his family. Krishna allows himself to be drawn in, partly by friendship with Yudhishthir's brother Arjuna; the sacred text known as the *Bhagavad Gita*, Song of the Blessed Lord, is in the form of a dialogue between them. When the conflict breaks out into open war, Krishna attaches himself to the Pandavas as a non-combatant adviser. It is fairly obvious that the side Krishna supports will win, however non-combatant he is. He saves Yudhishthir's outnumbered army with timely interventions, including miracles, and restores him to the kingship.

But the parallel is not very close. The Pandavas, if not their adversaries, always recognise Krishna's full divinity. He supports them for reasons of his own going far beyond the dynastic dispute. Righteousness is declining in India, and the victory of the Pandavas over their unscrupulous enemies is vital to its recovery. Krishna makes no attempt to stop the carnage, which his divine plan actually envisages, as an awestruck Arjuna learns in the *Gita*.

Merlin stands alone, and there is nobody like him. In Chapter 6 I assembled a few facts that suggest what his mythic origins might have been. There is no need to go over them again. But the following may serve as a reconstruction, a story — no more — that covers the facts.

The Britons, let us say, had a paramount god who was comparable to Apollo — who was, among other things, a god of inspiration and prophecy, as Apollo was. Britain was (as the Welsh text says) his 'precinct' or *temenos*, and he was Britain's tutelary deity. That belief was possible because Britain, exceptionally, was an island, sharply defined by its coasts and encircling sea. And so the cult of Britain's god could be uniquely Britain-oriented. Geography gave him a kind of personality.

He had a special association with Moridunum, and thus acquired the sobriquet Myrddin, which applied both to himself and to those inspired by him. Ambrosius and Lailoken were Myrddin-men, or, simply, Myrddins. Geoffrey of Monmouth picked up the sobriquet, and, for his own reason, made the change to 'Merlin'.

To the natural question 'Was Merlin a real person?', the most plausible answer is that there were several Merlins, perhaps many. We know one in Wales and one in Scotland. But if we want a Merlin *par excellence*, the original of the main legend, the place to look is Dinas Emrys. Here the Merlin who speaks the prophecies is localised at a place which is known to have been occupied at the right time by someone who could be identical with him. Here the story joins hands with archaeology. That may be pure coincidence, but there was *somebody* there, Ambrosius or Emrys perhaps, after whom the hill-fort was named.

As to Merlin's final fate, preference is a matter of taste. We are told that when Vortigern and his court evacuated the hill, Merlin took possession of it. Hence, perhaps, the material traces unearthed by excavation. However, he is not said to have made a permanent home there. Legend traces him in several directions, to several eventual ends, after his triumphant years as royal adviser and magician. He dies at Marlborough and is buried under an inordinately big mound. Or, thanks to the damsel, he passes into suspended animation in Cornwall or Brittany.

But the Welsh have another story, more attractive and more appropriate. Merlin is alive and well, and living on Bardsey Island.

Bardsey – Ynys Enlli in Welsh – is off the tip of the Lleyn peninsula, across Bardsey Sound. It is a mile and a half long, and has a steep hill on its eastern side. A Celtic monastery was founded here in the sixth century, and there are still some remains of medieval buildings. For a long time this island was a place of pilgrimage. According to legend, twenty thousand monks are buried here, but this is an exaggeration. Sometimes cowled ghosts are seen wandering on the shore. They are portents of storm and shipwreck.

Merlin's retirement to Bardsey was voluntary, not due to any enchantment, female or otherwise. His dwelling is an invisible house of glass, his *Ty Gwydr*. Some say he is asleep, as some say Arthur is, but he may not be. If awake and active, he is not alone: he has nine companions.

He is the guardian of the Thirteen Treasures of the Island of Britain – things of power that embody Britain's ancestral magic. In a time of trouble they were dispersed among several possessors, but Merlin persuaded them to hand over the Treasures to him for safe-keeping, and he took them to his House of Glass where they still are. Among them are the Chessboard of Gweddolau, with silver pieces on a board of gold, that play whole games by themselves without human agency; the Chariot of Morgan the Wealthy, which, without horses, will take a passenger swiftly to any destination; and the Sword of Rhydderch the Generous, that bursts into flame if a well-bred person draws it (he was called 'the generous' because he never objected to other people handling his sword, but they were afraid to try). There is a cloak of invisibility that once belonged to Arthur himself. There is the red coat of Padarn, which only a person of the right birth and disposition can put on. There are horns of plenty that pour out unlimited food and drink, and there are talismanic objects that test valour and virtue. Merlin is taking care of these timeless marvels in the House of Glass, out of the reach of Saxons and other marauders. No one knows what they look like, and they may have the same shape-shifting qualities as their custodian. Today we might be tempted to speak of three of them as the Chess Computer, the Car and the Laser Weapon.

Finally, some say that Merlin also has the true throne of Britain, and will enthrone Arthur when the king returns. Who else, indeed, would have that right?

Appendix:
The Continuing Encounter

A personal note may be in order here. *Merlin* is the belated outcome of a long involvement with British legend, especially Arthurian legend, in all its aspects: literary, historical, archaeological. While far from being an obsession, it has been for me a persistent and continuing interest, and several resulting books are listed under my name in the Bibliography at the end of this one. Over the years it has been a pleasure and an honour to discuss Arthurian topics with people of various interests, and sometimes with other writers, occasionally offering suggestions for books of their own. Such contacts have been made while lecturing in America and conducting groups around legendary sites in Britain.

It has always been part of this legend's enduring strength that King Arthur does not stand by himself. With him are Queen Guinevere and the Knights of the Round Table. He is not the kind of hero whom folklorists classify as a loner: he presides over a vividly imagined group. These legendary figures weave such a spell that countless readers have suspected an element of reality in at least some of them, and have theorised and argued over attempts to establish what it is. Was Arthur a real historical person, or, at least, did his legend originate in such a person? My own reflections have led me to what I believe is at least a

223

partial answer, and *The Discovery of King Arthur* is there for anyone to read.

But the name of Arthur evokes another. Beside him is the prophet and wonder-worker who presided at his birth, who made him king, and who stood by him during the first turbulent phases of his reign. Until the tragedy that parts them, Merlin is Arthur's great companion. He too fascinates readers, yet he is even more elusive. To echo the question just posed, is Merlin a real historical person, however mythified? Or is he pure fantasy?

It was clear to me long ago that his story could not be told as even a conjectural biography. Yet it might still be possible to follow it as bards and romancers developed it; to see how Merlin took shape in literary and popular imagination; and to judge whether any historical reality does emerge. That is what I have tried to do in this book, but belatedly. I considered the idea before, but dropped it. Why?

Chiefly because such a medley of authors, medieval and modern, had seen Merlin's potential as a character and developed it in different ways. Their flights of fancy might begin with the authentic traditions (well, more or less) but they branched off in different directions. They put Merlin in the remote past or the remote future; they put him in science-fiction; they endowed him with incredible power and influence; they made him a story-book companion for children; they plunged him into unprecedented adventures and love-affairs. By the late twentieth century the Merlin saga, surveyed as a whole, was impossible to discuss as a whole. And I preferred not to try.

Yet Merlin would not quite leave me alone. A few gracious and amusing sentences by one of his novelists brought me, after a fashion, face to face with him. Persia Woolley wrote *Child of the Northern Spring*, telling the story of the young Guinevere as a first-person narrative. Towards the end she is awaiting Arthur at Glastonbury near the foot of the Tor, the sacred mountain. She knows that Merlin is nearby with his friend Nimue: 'Apple trees heavy with fruit covered the lower flank of the Tor, and as I entered the orchard, Nimue's laughter came lightly from a little house hidden within it. It seemed that Merlin had chosen a fitting spot for his nest.' Persia/Guinevere's topography is exact throughout the passage. She knew where Merlin was. She located him (I hasten to say, with my approval) in my own home, Chalice Orchard. After that, for me, it remained his confidential retreat. It wasn't, of course, another 221B Baker Street, even for me, but the legend had touched it.

In a final delayed approach to the mysterious topic, I decided that the only way to get it under control, without the aforesaid complications, was to divide it. As readers will have seen, the main body of this book traces the evolution of the legend, the growth of Merlin as a character, his possible historical aspect, and the principal treatments of him in literature, down to recent times. But I appreciate that it is not enough; it is not quite fair. In this Appendix, I recognise various fictions, films, poems and so on which also introduce Merlin and which it would have been wrong to pass over in silence; however, they are outside the mainstream, and would have caused confusion if I had tried to involve them directly. Some are worth more than a glance – some, much more.

Here is my supplementary list, with a word about each item.

Books

Apollinaire, Guillaume, *L'Enchanteur Pourrissant* (Paris: Minard, 1922)
Merlin, imprisoned, has visions of characters from different mythologies.
Barjavel, René, *L'Enchanteur* (Paris: Denoel, 1984)
Merlin's preparation for the Grail Quest.
Bidder, George, *Merlin's Youth* (Westminster: Constable, 1899)
A narrative poem in which Merlin learns magic from a sinister woman. He defeats the Britons' enemies, but is condemned for doing it by unhallowed means.
Binyon, Laurence, *The Madness of Merlin* (London: Macmillan, 1947)
Poetic development of the conception of Merlin as an inspired madman in Geoffrey of Monmouth's Vita Merlini.
Clare, Helen, *Merlin's Magic* (London: Lane, 1953)
Story for children about meetings with Arthurian characters.
Colum, Padraic, *The Boy Apprenticed to an Enchanter* (New York: Macmillan, 1920)
Story for children about Merlin rescuing a boy from an evil wizard.
Craig, Alec, *The Voice of Merlin* (London: Fortune, 1946)
Poetic drama portraying a Merlin who deceives and exploits.
Dane, Clemence, *The Saviours* (London and Toronto: Heinemann, 1942)
Radio plays about British national heroes, with Merlin as narrator.
Fry, Christopher, *Thor, with Angels* (London: Oxford University Press, 1949)
Verse drama in which Merlin talks of a Christian reawakening in England.
Furst, Clyde B., *Merlin* (New York, 1930)

A blank-verse poem in which the magician rises above his inner conflicts and becomes a public benefactor.

Hildebrandt, Rita and Tim, *Merlin and the Dragons of Atlantis* (Indianapolis and New York: Bobbs-Merrill, 1983)

A science-fiction novel set in the distant past, when Atlantis and Lemuria still existed. Merlin's skills and the dragons are produced by the sciences of the lost continents.

Howells, Graham, *Merlin Awakes* (Llandysul, Ceredigion: Pont Books, 2003)

Junior story with cartoon-type illustrations, including Welsh legends, some from the Mabinogion.

Lawhead, Stephen R., *Merlin* (Westchester, Illinois: Crossway, 1988)

Second in a trilogy of fantasy novels based on Welsh legend. Merlin, taught by Taliesin, is preparing the way for Arthur.

Muir, Edwin, *Merlin*, in Muir, *Collected Poems* (Oxford: Oxford University Press, 1965)

A poem evoking a lost age of magic.

Newman, Robert, *Merlin's Mistake* (New York: Atheneum, 1970)

Junior fantasy about a boy whom Merlin has mistakenly gifted with knowledge of the future.

Nye, Robert, *Merlin* (London: Hamish Hamilton, 1978)

Farcical version of the Arthurian legend, with surreal sexual fantasy; narrated by Merlin from his crystal cave.

San Souci, Robert D., *Young Merlin* (Yearling, 1996)

Junior presentation of Merlin's early life before he met Arthur.

Skinner, Martyn, *The Return of Arthur* (London: Chapman & Hall, 1966)

A two-part comic epic in the manner of Byron's Don Juan. *Arthur, brought back by Merlin, saves Europe from Marxist domination.*

Trevor, Meriol, *Merlin's Ring* (London: Collins, 1957)
Junior fantasy about a boy transported into the past by the power of the magician's ring. He witnesses events leading up to Arthur's principal victory, but the Britons' behaviour is disillusioning.
Yolen, Jane, *Merlin and the Dragons* (Picture Puffins, 1996)
Adventures of Arthur as a boy, aided by Merlin; introduces the theme of the fighting dragons.

Films

Excalibur. Warner Brothers, 1981. Directed by John Boorman.
Interprets major Arthurian stories and offers a serious portrayal of Merlin as a transitional figure between paganism and Christianity.
Merlin. Hallmark Entertainment, 1998. Made for television.
Presents Merlin as mature during the main action, and deeply involved with events in Geoffrey of Monmouth's History. *Non-Arthurian characters are added, notably Queen Mab, a sinister enchantress who hopes to exploit Merlin's powers, but whom he opposes.*
Three books by James Mallory form a trilogy of the film: *Merlin: the Old Magic* (Warner Books, 1999); *Merlin: The King's Wizard* (Warner Books, 1999); and *Merlin: the End of Magic* (Warner Books, 2000).

Graphic Novel

Barr, Mike W. and Bolland, Brian, *Camelot 3000* (New York: DC Comics, 1988)
The main Arthurian characters reappear (one or two of them curiously changed) to combat an alien threat to Earth.

bibliography

Alcock, Leslie. 'Wales in the Arthurian Age', in Geoffrey Ashe (ed.), *The Quest for Arthur's Britain* (London: Pall Mall Press, 1968)

Alcock, Leslie, Stevenson, S.J. and Musson, C.R. *Cadbury Castle, Somerset: The Early Medieval Archaeology* (Cardiff: University of Wales Press, 1995)

Annales Cambriae. See Nennius

Ashe, Geoffrey. *Avalonian Quest* (London: Methuen, 1982)

———. *The Book of Prophecy* (London: Orion, 2002)

———. *The Discovery of King Arthur* (Stroud: Sutton Publishing, 2005)

———. *Merlin* (Newton Toney: Wessex Books, 2001)

———. *Mythology of the British Isles*, revised edn (London: Methuen, 2002)

———. *The Traveller's Guide to Arthurian Britain* (Glastonbury: Gothic Image Publications, 1997)

Bannerman, Anne. 'The Prophecy of Merlin', in Alan and Barbara Lupack (eds), *Arthurian Literature by Women* (New York: Garland, 1999)

Brinkley, Roberta F. *Arthurian Legend in the Seventeenth Century*, new edn (New York: Octagon Press, 1966)

Bromwich, Rachel. *Trioedd Ynys Prydein*, the Welsh Triads, with translation and notes, 2nd edn (Cardiff: University of Wales Press, 1978)

Brown, Peter. *The World of Late Antiquity* (London: Thames, 1971)

Bryant, Nigel (ed. and trans.) *Merlin and the Grail: the romances attributed to Robert de Boron* (Cambridge: D.S. Brewer, 2003)

Carley, James P. *Glastonbury Abbey* (Woodbridge: Boydell, 1988)

Chadwick, N. K. *Early Brittany* (Cardiff: University of Wales Press, 1969)

Chambers, E.K. *Arthur of Britain* (London: Sidgwick, 1927)

Chippindale, Christopher. *Stonehenge Complete* (London: Thames & Hudson, 1983)

Chrétien de Troyes. *Arthurian Romances*, trans. with an introduction by William W. Kibler and Carleton W. Carroll (Harmondsworth: Penguin Books, 1991)

Clancy, Joseph P. *The Earliest Welsh Poetry* (London: Macmillan, 1970)

Collingwood, R.G. and Myres, J.N.L. *Roman Britain and the English Settlements*, 2nd edn (London and New York: Oxford, 1937)

Dames, Michael. *Merlin and Wales: A Magician's Landscape* (London: Thames & Hudson, 2002)

Duggan, Alfred. *Conscience of the King* (New York: Coward-McCann, 1951)

Fletcher, Robert Huntington. *The Arthurian Material in the Chronicles*, 2nd edn (New York: Franklin, 1966)

Geoffrey of Monmouth. *The Historia Regum Britannie of Geoffrey of Monmouth*, Latin ed. Neil Wright (Cambridge: D.S. Brewer, 1984)

——. *The History of the Kings of Britain*, trans. with an introduction by Lewis Thorpe (London: Penguin, 1966)

——. *Vita Merlini* (The Life of Merlin), trans. John J. Parry, in Peter Goodrich (ed.), *The Romance of Merlin* (New York: Garland, 1990)

Gerald of Wales (otherwise Giraldus Cambrensis). *The Journey Through Wales* and *The Description of Wales*, trans. Lewis Thorpe (Harmondsworth: Penguin Books, 1978)

Gildas. *The Ruin of Britain*, in *History from the Sources*, vol. 7, ed. and trans. Michael Winterbottom (Chichester: Phillimore, 1978)

Goodrich, Peter (ed.) *The Romance of Merlin* (New York: Garland, 1990)

Graves, Robert. *The White Goddess*, amended and enlarged edn (London: Faber & Faber, 1952)

Greenlaw, Edwin. *Studies in Spenser's Historical Allegory*, new edn (New York: Octagon Press, 1966)

Hale, Amy, Kent, Alan M. and Saunders, Tim (eds) *Inside Merlin's Cave* (London: Boutle, 2000)

Harvey, P.D.H. *Mappa Mundi: The Hereford World Map* (Hereford Cathedral and the British Library, 1996)

Jarman, A.O.H. 'The Merlin Legend and the Welsh Tradition of Prophecy', in *The Arthur of the Welsh*, ed. Rachel Bromwich, A.O.H. Jarman and Brynley F. Roberts (Cardiff: University of Wales Press, 1991)

Lacy, Norris J. (ed.) *The New Arthurian Encyclopedia* (New York: Garland, 1991)

——. with Geoffrey Ashe and Debra Mancoff. *The Arthurian Handbook*, 2nd edn (New York: Garland, 1997)

Lewis, C.S. *That Hideous Strength*, in *The Cosmic Trilogy* (London: Macmillan, 1989)

Loomis, R.S. (ed.) *Arthurian Literature in the Middle Ages* (London: Oxford, The Clarendon Press, 1959; New York: Oxford, 1959)

The Mabinogion, trans. with an introduction by Jeffrey Gantz (Harmondsworth: Penguin, 1976)

Malory, Sir Thomas. *Le Morte d'Arthur*, ed. with modernised spelling by Janet Cowan. 2 vols (Harmondsworth: Penguin, 1969)

Mason, Eugene (trans.) *Arthurian Chronicles* (including the Arthurian portion of Wace) (London: Dent, 1962)

Nennius. *British History*, in *History from the Sources*, vol. 8 (including the *Annales Cambriae*), ed. and trans. John Morris (Chichester: Phillimore, 1980)

Piggott, Stuart. *The Druids* (London: Penguin, 1974)

The Quest of the Holy Grail, trans. P.M. Matarosso (London: Penguin, 1969)

Quinet, Edgar. *Merlin l'Enchanteur*, 2 vols (Paris: Librairie Hachette, 1895)

——. *Histoire d'un Enfant*, trans. as *The Story of a Child* by Rosemary and Peter Ganz (London: Duckworth, 1995)

Robert de Boron. See Bryant

Robinson, Edwin Arlington. *Merlin* (1917), in Peter Goodrich (ed.), *The Romance of Merlin* (New York: Garland, 1990)

Ross, Anne. *Pagan Celtic Britain* (London: Routledge, 1967, and Sphere, 1974)

Rowley, William. *The Birth of Merlin*, text with discussions by Harold F. Brooks, R.J. Stewart, Denise Coffey and Roy Hudd (Shaftesbury: Element Books, 1989)

Snyder, Christopher. *Exploring the World of King Arthur* (London: Thames & Hudson, 2000)

Spenser, Edmund. *The Faerie Queene*, in *Poetical Works*, ed. J.C. Smith and E. de Selincourt (London: Oxford University Press, 1912)

Spivak, Charlotte (ed.) *Merlin Versus Faust: Contending Archetypes in Western Culture* (Lewiston, New York: The Edward Millen Press, 1992)

Stewart, Mary. *The Crystal Cave* (1970), *The Hollow Hills* (1973) and *The Last Enchantment* (1979) (London: Hodder & Stoughton)

Stewart, R.J. (ed.) *The Book of Merlin* (Poole: The Blandford Press, 1987)

Sutcliff, Rosemary. *Sword at Sunset* (London: Hodder & Stoughton, 1963)

Tennyson, Alfred Lord. *Idylls of the King*, ed. J.M. Gray (London: Penguin Books, 1996)

Thomas, Charles. 'Tintagel Castle', in *Antiquity*, LXII (September 1988)

Tolstoy, Nikolai. *The Quest for Merlin* (London: Hamish Hamilton, 1985)

Twain, Mark. *A Connecticut Yankee in King Arthur's Court*, with Afterword by Edmund Reiss (New York: New American Library, 1963)

Wace. See Mason

Westwood, Jennifer, and Simpson, Jacqueline. *The Lore of the Land* (London: Penguin Books, 2005)

White, T.H. *The Once and Future King* (London: Collins, 1958)

Woolley, Persia. *Child of the Northern Spring* (New York: Poseidon Press, 1987)

Wordsworth, William. *The Poetical Works of William Wordsworth*, vol. 3, ed. E. de Selincourt and Helen Darbishire (Oxford: Clarendon, 1954)

INDEX